Fun With Bible Geography

Marie Chapman

ACCENT BOOKS

Denver, Colorado

MEMBER OF
EVANGELICAL CHRISTIAN
PUBLISHERS ASSOCIATION

ACCENT BOOKS
A division of Accent-B/P Publications, Inc.
12100 W. Sixth Avenue
P.O. Box 15337
Denver, Colorado 80215

Library of Congress Catalog Card Number: 80-65055
ISBN 0-89636-044-X

WHATEVER AGE YOU TEACH ...
you will teach the Bible better if
you have a good knowledge of the
lands and customs that form the
background of Bible events. With
this book you can make teaching
Bible Geography actually fun!

Fun
With Bible
Geography

Contents

Preface

Some masterful volumes have been published to wrap up the history and geography of the Holy Land. In-depth consideration has been given to the heritage of the Bible student. Some of these fine books are included in the last chapter of this book.

It is not the purpose of this author to add particularly to the factual knowledge concerning the length and breadth nor climate and customs of the lands of the Bible. The purpose is rather to get some of that knowledge transferred from the pages of those books into the hearts and minds of Sunday School teachers and pupils.

"How many of you have not referred to the maps at the back of your Bible in a Sunday School class for as long as a year?" I asked a class of mature Bible Institute students.

"Make it twelve!" retorted a young man on the front row.

Alas, his commentary is too accurate. Furthermore, many teachers and students alike want to keep it that way. In a single week awhile ago, I taught a workshop in Bible Geography in two different national Sunday School conventions. Both had smaller attendance than other workshops. Discussion at those workshops uncovered the fact that the teachers present admittedly knew little about "the lay of the land" themselves and had not been in the habit of stressing geography facts in their teaching. But of course they cannot teach what they do not know.

This book will point out some highlights of Holy Land geography, but its chief aim is to make the learning of those facts not only interesting but actual *fun.*

"Geography . . . fun? You've got to be kidding!" someone exclaims.

Try it and see.

MARIE CHAPMAN
Amherst, Virginia

The sources and prices of resource materials given make this book of special value to teachers who desire to help Bible geography come alive for their students. The prices, however, may change and are given here only to show the price range of the items presented.

1
Why Bother About Geography?

Why should we who teach Bible lessons be concerned about where David killed the giant? Do pupils need to know where the whale was when Jonah got swallowed? There are a number of good reasons why a teacher should stress the locale and customs of Bible stories.

To See the Setting of a Lesson

Knowledge of setting lends reality to a story—true or fictional. In 1919, page 1 of Harold Bell Wright's *The Recreation of Brian Kent* began with the author describing the first meeting with Auntie Sue, a chief character. Before we know what color eyes she had, what age she was, or whether she smiled a lot, we are introduced to her surroundings. We felt we knew her: we'd been to her house.

In 1976, page 1 of Marti Hefley's *In His Steps Today* (Moody Press) introduces Heather Novak. We begin at once to identify with Heather, because the author paints a word picture of exactly where Heather is and what she is doing.

Back up to another "golden oldie" in Gene Stratton-Porter's *Freckles,* reprinted in 1965. We *see* Freckles walking down a woodland road, and we feel the cool beauty of the scene—long before we know where Freckles got his name.

Those three authors are considered superior in their craft. The sales records and longevity of the books attest to their expertise. And they felt it was necessary to describe where their characters lived and solved their problems.

Today's fiction writers like to be more subtle than the

old masters. No more long pages of description to slow down the progress of the plot. Instead, descriptive facts are woven into the story bit by bit. Economy of words characterizes necessary scenario.

The Bible is likewise characterized by economy of words. There are no long and flowery descriptive passages. Look at Genesis 11, for instance. Noah and his family are out of the ark. Verse 2 says they journeyed east and "found a plain in the land of Shinar and settled there." That's all. We can guess from verse 3 that there was some kind of clay suitable for making bricks. We can guess that there must not have been many stones, since bricks were a substitute. We can guess there was a source of tar. Would that source be a tree? From verse 4, we can infer that they felt sure of an inexhaustible supply of these building materials. They planned for that tower to go to heaven.

And exactly where is Shinar in relation to anywhere we have been before in the Bible narrative? Was it a long ways from the Garden of Eden? How far did the ark actually travel from where it started? And where *did* it start from?

To Know Bible Places

Young children today begin learning about the contemporary world in school. Granted, some are like the boy in a cartoon. Two kids are approaching the school's front door and one is saying to the other: "I've finally learned all the 50 capitals, but I have no idea which states they're in." Nevertheless, he was making progress.

Bible places often have different names today. If school students have learned modern names of places mentioned in the Bible, they still might not be able to make the transfer to Bible events. Because the effort is most apt to be made in Sunday School, it is vital that a teacher include knowledge of Bible places.

One example of this name change is Cana, in which city (John 2) Jesus turns the water into wine. Today the town is called Kefer-Kanna. If you did not know you were looking for a town by the latter name, a modern map would not be helpful.

Again, Old Testament Accho (Judges 1:31) was in the New Testament called Ptolemais (Acts 21:7) and was the

Crusaders' capital city. The historically famous town is now called Akko.

Acts 9:32-35 tells of Peter's healing Aeneas at Lydda. The city was called Lod in Nehemiah 7:37 and other Old Testament passages, and it is called Lod today, a place near modern Tel Aviv.

If it is important for children to know all the new independent countries of Africa and the chief exports of Spain, it is important for them to know where a Bible city was during Bible days and whether it still bears the same name.

Adults who tour the Holy Land also do well to be armed with a copy of a guide such as Guy Duffield's *Handbook of Bible Lands* (Regal; see Chapter 11 for ordering information). Otherwise, when a tour guide points out Zefat, northeast of the Sea of Galilee, he will not know he is looking at Safad. Many believe it was Safad to which Jesus referred when He spoke of the "city set on a hill." It was one of the cities important to the Jews.

To Understand Life in Bible Times

Television affords armchair travel never before possible with such realism and such universal accessibility. Life in another land comes into the living room with a flick of a knob. With TV introduction, church families should seek to know more about what life was like in Bible times, to understand that the men and women in their Sunday School lessons were people like themselves.

What kind of picture is conjured in your mind when you read of the lad who brought a lunch of "five loaves of bread and two fishes" (Matthew 14:17)? Unless a previous exposure to the story has clarified the concept of "bread" in Bible times, a child hearing the story needs to know more than simply that there were "five loaves and two fishes." To a child in western countries, the boy might seem to have an unusually large lunch if it contained five loaves of bread such as he sees stacked on the shelves of the supermarket. He needs to know that the lunch contained what were really five biscuits or rolls. The fish were also small.

Notice another puzzle in the Luke 2 account of Jesus' trip to Jerusalem at age 12 (verse 42). It says they "went up" to Jerusalem. A casual glance at a map of the Holy

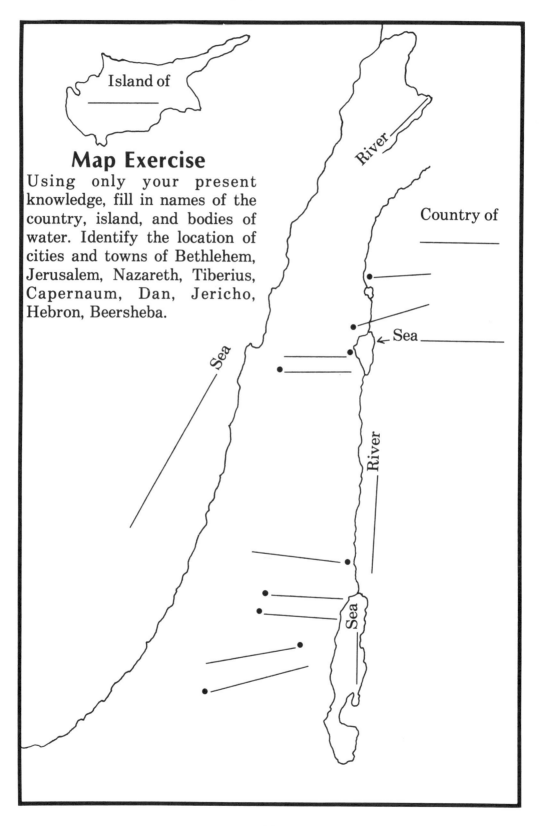

Island of
_____

Map Exercise

Using only your present knowledge, fill in names of the country, island, and bodies of water. Identify the location of cities and towns of Bethlehem, Jerusalem, Nazareth, Tiberius, Capernaum, Dan, Jericho, Hebron, Beersheba.

River

Country of
_____

_____

Sea

← Sea _____

_____

River

Sea

Land in the time of Christ will show that Jerusalem is south of Nazareth, where Jesus lived at that age. How, then, could they be said to go *up*? And how, in verse 51, for the return trip, could Jesus be said to go "down" with them? The answer lies in knowing that from anywhere in the land, pilgrims must go *up* to reach the holy city of Jerusalem, for it is built on hills. What seems like an error on the part of the narrator is clear enough in the light of that geographical fact.

To Understand Bible Facts

The word *geography* frightens away people who had difficulty remembering names of cities and rivers during a six-weeks test. The word itself can be studiously avoided, while the geographical facts are interwoven in lesson presentation.

For example, in II Kings 6:24 the story begins about the siege of Samaria. How far did the Syrians travel? (Can you show the distance on a wall map? Do students have maps in their Bibles or pupil's books? This research is an occasion when a map should be used.) That army went some little distance, probably on foot, in order to get to the destination. What kind of land did they traverse? What route did they take?

Actually, there are many interesting ways today to make learning geography facts a pleasure. Watch for them and use them in your teaching.

Look at the blank map in the Map Exercise. Can you put the correct names beside the dots? If not, perhaps you will want to make sure your pupils will not be equally at a loss in days to come. (Fill in names of the countries, bodies of water, and cities as far as you can now. Add others as you learn more about these countries.)

Before we go on to explore new ways to enjoy learning about Bible places and customs, the next chapter will examine some facts about the Lands of the Bible.

2
Looking at the Bible Lands

While the purpose of this book is not to present a course in geography, per se, but to motivate and expedite its mastery, a brief look at the Bible lands is in order. Let us view them as an armchair tour of Bible lands.

"My trip to the Holy Land really made the Bible come alive for me!" enthusiastic tourists exclaim. Why? Doubtless because for the first time they really comprehended that Bible places are real places. They gained perspective by which to measure distances between cities mentioned in Bible stories. They acquired firsthand knowledge of the rugged hills and rocky terrain, to compare them with familiar areas at home. They could say with authority: "David needed mighty men in his volunteer army—weaklings could never have survived the hard life on that rocky land!"

After such a glimpse of the Lands of the Bible, it is true that Bible stories become "His-story," enacted in real places with real names. While the houses and streets of cities may be on the third or fourth stratum of civilization in a given site, the town may be set in the same general area where Jesus ministered, such as Bethany, or where Abraham sojourned, like Hebron.

Too bad all teachers can't afford a trip like that, isn't it! The fact is that, for far less than the hundreds of dollars a round trip flight would cost, any Bible teacher *can* go for an armchair tour of Bible Lands—avoiding lack of sleep, extreme heat, insects, a strange diet and impure water. Here's how:

1. Invest $3.00 in the map called "Lands of the Bible Today," from National Geographic Society. (A complete list of sources and addresses is given at back of book.)

2. Order GAF's Viewmaster reels (GAF Corporation) entitled "Holy Land" (B226) and "Modern Israel" (B244),

at $1.80 each. Of course, if you don't have a Viewmaster, you can buy one for less than $3.00 at many department stores or toy stores—or order from GAF.

First, open your big new map and keep it open on a folding table near your chair. You will want to refer to it as we travel, to find (a) names of places, as used in Bible times and now; (b) Scripture references of events that happened at many of the places; (c) rivers; (d) mountains; (e) historical events.

Keep the Viewmaster handy, too. As you "visit" each place, look to see which reel shows that picture and enjoy a 3-D look at it.

There is one good feature about this tour that would not be true of a whirlwind ten-day tour overseas: You can ask the guide to repeat the facts as many times as you wish, without boring anyone else or being told it is time to rush away to something else. If things move too fast to absorb the facts the first time, you can have as many reruns as you need.

Cyprus

From whatever place on the globe your trip originates, for the purpose of this tour your plane will land at a spot in the midst of the Mediterranean Sea—Nicosia, on Cyprus. (You will find it at E-8 on your map.) We need not be detained at Passport Clearance on an armchair tour.

It is a strange feeling to ride down the road toward Famagusta (Fah-mah-goose'tah) in the hollow of the east-coast crescent Famagusta Bay. The bus is rushing down the left side of the road and you are meeting cars which whiz past on your right. Quite dizzying, in fact, unless you come from England. But you may concentrate on the glimpses of people and houses, all so "foreign-looking." You get the feeling that some people you pass are equally amused at the sight of the busload of gawking passengers of such an assortment of sizes, colors, and shapes. "People-watching" is not confined to the intruders.

For this tour, we shall enjoy the unique experience of spending our nights on a "floating hotel," a Greek ship we shall call the *Orpheus*. Walk up the gangplank at Famagusta and get your stateroom located. It will be a day or two before you get your days and nights into their new orbit. There is a time difference of at least seven hours, you find.

Turkey

You are rocked to sleep on a moving ship, and —Presto!—in the morning you get out of bed in Turkey. Find Mersin on the southern coast of Turkey (about D-9), straight above Famagusta.

Just be glad you don't *really* have to wait till the end of your breakfast before your coffee is served—you can drink it first, if you wish, in your armchair. Braced by a good continental breakfast, let's move along down the gangplank and join the crowds boarding the tour buses to take us from place to place. Note the number of your bus; when they count noses, they will be distressed if yours is not among those on board.

Let's move eastward along the map, leaving our port city of 120,000 people, and speed down the "wrong side" of a road that doesn't approach your concept of an interstate highway. Look off to the left: three Turkish women in baggy trousers are walking slowly down a road that resembles an alley, each bent under a large load of faggots.

First stop, Tarsus. Find it there, about an inch east of Mersin? (That's 45 miles, says the map.) At the birthplace of Paul, the guide explains that "This is a city as old as humanity, built by the sons of Adam more than 8,000 years ago."

Do you see the Taurus Mountains? Those same mountains were beheld daily by young Saul of Tarsus. Now, which would you rather do: Follow the crowd as one of a herd of sheep and look for a moment at a church where Saul possibly attended in youth? Or stay near the buses and take pictures of the beautiful black-eyed children and the curious-looking women with those baggy trousers? Nearby, you can see adobe houses with piles of faggots by the door—possibly brought there by the three women you saw. You think you are observing *them,* till you look at the high, flat-roofed building across the road and see that more and more men and boys seem to be gathering on the roof, looking down at *you.* It could be time to find the rest of the crowd, after all . . . .

You find them at the Cleopatra Gate, the one that famous beauty rode through for her first meeting with Mark Antony. The gate dates back to 300 B.C. If you inquire why buildings and walls stand up so long, you learn that in Turkey (and in much of the Middle East) there is little rainfall and almost no snow. Therefore, moisture to mold or disintegrate building materials is no problem.

Possibly the hardness of the ground accounts for the lack of clothes poles. Even where there are large open spaces near a house, the clothes may be seen drying on the roof. (In cities, watch for clotheslines strung from window to window, so that the building exterior becomes colorful with drying clothes.)

We speed on through Adana, a city much larger than Mersin, but of little biblical significance. For Americans, it is recognized as the site of an American air base. The "feel" of a Moslem land penetrates, as minarets begin to flavor the local color. You learn that in Turkey there are 37 million people, 95 percent of whom are Moslem. The devout adherents to that faith shame prayerless church members who watch them when the *muezzin* steps onto the balcony of a minaret and raises his shofar (ram's horn or megaphone—more recently an electric public address system microphone) to shout, "Allah is one God and we are his people!" and invoke them to pray. And pray, they do, reminded thus five times a day. They stop buses, get out prayer rugs and kneel where they are; facing Mecca, they pray to Allah.

Heading east and then south along the coast, we will pass through places once conquered by Alexander the Great, to stop after 75 miles for lunch at a seaport town called Iskenderun (once Alexandretta). From the contents of the Greek lunch sack provided by the ship's steward, you may choose the food which seems most like home and discard the rest—the waiting gangs of hungry children will see that no food is left to litter the outdoor tearoom where you are. Be sure to take a look at the beautiful leather bags for sale and to raise your eyes to the snowcapped Taurus Mountains behind the city.

In St. Paul Country, we will stop about 35 miles farther down the coast at a site of special significance in his life: Antakya. Of course you don't know it by that name. In

Paul's day it was Antioch, the place where he and Barnabas ministered, where the disciples were first derisively called "Christians."

Their church, called "St. Peter's Church," is actually a cave where the early Christians met, ready to evacuate at a moment's notice via a rear passage hewn out of the limestone rock.

Outside, look down the hillside, where shepherds are watching their sheep, and consider the city of 61,000 people. Ponder the meaning of the many minarets piercing the sky. Notice the variety of conveyances on the streets: carts, horse-drawn-two-wheel buggy taxis, bicycles, automobiles and buses.

Modern Antioch.

Lebanon

Let's travel south 150 miles along the coast now, to rejoin the floating hotel, docked at Beirut, Lebanon. The next morning, bright and early, we go up the hill from the city by the sea. We are in Aley, where we note the large, fine houses all shuttered up. These, we learn, are the summer homes of the wealthy families of Beirut, who will move up the hill to occupy them when the heat rises to 120 in the lowlands. Notice the blue trim painted around windows and doors? "That's to keep out the evil eye," our guide informs us.

Our tour bus takes us fifty miles northeast of Beirut to Baalbek, the "City of the Sun." Our map tells us that here stand temple remains that are the most imposing of the Roman world, not excluding Rome itself. Located at the edge of the vast plain of Bekaa, Baalbek actually means to the Jew "Lord of the Bekaa." Begun in 28 B.C. under Augustus, construction of temples to the various Roman deities continued 250 years.

Ruins in Baalbek, Lebanon.

Most visitors to Baalbek come back home with a picture of themselves dwarfed by the mighty columns of the ruined pagan temples. Human figures in a picture provide perspective for judging the immensity of the ancient structures. Besides the enormous places of worship in varying stages of ruin, the "Midi stone" is a major attraction. We learn that this stone weighs several tons and probably required 40,000 men to move it a short distance and raise it into position.

Syria

We lunch and board buses to go 100 miles southeast to "the oldest continuously inhabited city"—Damascus, dating back to 2,000 B.C., the capital of Syria. First Bible mention of this city is in Genesis 14:15, where Abram pursued the captors of Lot to a point north of it. In II Samuel 8:5,6, it figures in David's warfare. It was one of the ten city-states in the area called the Decapolis.

One stop in Damascus is at the wall, where we see the window through which Paul was let down to safety (Acts 9:22-25). We also see the street called Straight (Acts 9:11).

Take off your shoes as we enter the Omayad Mosque, once the Church of St. John the Baptist. That funereal structure in the center, says the guide, is "where the *head* of John the Baptist is buried."

Syria was the land of Naaman the Leper, who at first refused Elisha's instruction, preferring the clean waters of his own land, the Abana and Pharphar (II Kings 5), which flowed through and near Damascus.

Syria is usually considered by geographers as that portion of land bounded by the Taurus Mountains and the Euphrates River on the north, the Arabian Desert on the east, Palestine on the south, and the Mediterranean Sea on the west. The old Hebrew name for it, Aram, is rooted in the word for "height." The Lebanon Mountains span 100 miles on the west. Syria's population is something over five million today.

Mesopotamia

We won't have time to go to Mesopotamia on our make-believe buses—it's too far east. But in our armchair we don't need to cross the Syrian Desert; we can drop down onto the map and view briefly the "cradle of man."

Where did man first live on the earth? Where was the Garden of Eden? While Bible scholars agree on the general area, the exact location cannot be pinpointed. It was (according to Genesis 2:8-14) in the midst of four rivers, two of which are known: The Tigris (called Hiddekel in Genesis 2:14) and the Euphrates. The land was known as Mesopotamia, "land between the rivers." Today the country of Iraq occupies this area.

Both rivers flow from northwest to southeast—the

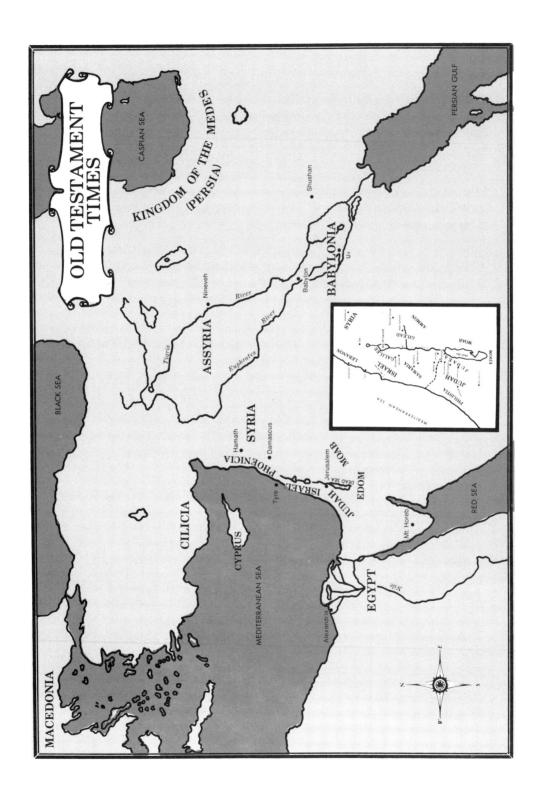

Euphrates about 1700 miles and the Tigris 1150. Today, because of centuries when silt was deposited at their mouths, the two rivers merge about 100 miles before they reach the Persian Gulf (about G-16, at Al Qurnah, on your map) and flow into the Gulf in a stream called Shatt al Arab. Because of the diagonal shape, the land measures 290 miles in length, northwest to southeast, and 300 miles east to west.

This land which had not known rainfall before the Flood (Genesis 2:5) knows comparatively little of it now. Even in the rainy season there may not be more than seven inches of rain, with little or none the rest of the year, though the northern section may have slightly more moisture. The Garden of Eden was "watered by the rivers." Sometimes the "land between the rivers" is flooded, but not to the benefit of the hard-baked ground. Instead, the raging waters may take with them a layer of dirt as well as the walls of mud houses.

Babylonia

The southern section of Mesopotamia is the plain of Shinar, also known as Babylonia (Genesis 10:8-10). The land near the Persian Gulf was once occupied by the Sumerians. Ancient Babylon was on the west bank of the Euphrates, about fifty miles south of modern Baghdad (on the Tigris at F-14), which dates back only to 1200 B.C.

Summer temperatures in this area may be as high as 108°F in the shade. With no shade it can go to 140°.

Through the years, various theories have been advanced by geologists and archaeologists concerning the exact site of ancient Babylon. The excavations of Robert Koldewey (1899-1917) resulted in a clear view of Babylon at the time of Nebuchadnezzar's splendor and defined the immensity of the city. Here and there over the plains, excavators have sought to identify various ziggurats with the Tower of Babel, from which Babylon got its name. Present-day scholars tend to believe it will be none of these, but one within the walls of the city, where evidence of a ziggurat can be distinguished in the ruins of the ancient city.

Like New Testament Capernaum, Babylon as an inhabited city is extinct. The destruction foretold in Scripture came upon both (Isaiah 13:19-22; Matthew 11:23).

Chaldea

You will find Chaldea in Lower Mesopotamia, beside modern Kuwait, which is at H-16 on the map, next to the Persian Gulf. When Abram was called forth from Ur of the Chaldees (Genesis 11:31; 12:1), he was not a nomad who merely folded his tent and moved on. He lived in an important city of his time. In the earliest day of Bible history Ur was the capital of the Sumerian Empire. It was on the west side of the Euphrates (you can locate the ruins at Tell el Obeid, near G-15 on your map).

The noted archaeologist, Sir Leonard Woolley, unearthed this area to reveal that in Abraham's day Ur was a great and prosperous city. He also restored the ancient ziggurat which figured in the worship of the moon god, which gives us a good idea of Abraham's surroundings when God called him.

Inventions which seem to us quite modern were in use among these people, who had developed a form of writing (cuneiform), owned chariots, and had a system of mathematics. Clay tablets of recent discovery record the Creation and the Flood stories.

Assyria

In the northern section of Iraq (formerly Mesopotamia), across the Tigris River and east of the city of Mosul, parts of the ancient Assyrian city of Nineveh have been uncovered in recent years (see E-13 on your map). Like Babylonia, the history of the Assyrians dates back to the descendants of Noah, through his son Ham (Genesis 10:11). In this relatively small area of northern Mesopotamia, between the Tigris and Zab rivers, the mighty empire of the Assyrians virtually dominated the civilized world during the ninth to seventh centuries B.C. Closely connected with the Babylonians in bloodline, the Assyrians at times controlled most of Mesopotamia; at other times the Babylonians rose to control.

In the eighth century B.C. the Assyrians invaded Israel and exacted tribute from the king of Israel (II Kings 15:19,20). Later, after besieging Samaria for three years, they conquered the Israelites and took captives back to Assyria (II Kings 17:4-6; I Chronicles 5:25,26).

The Assyrians were known for their extreme cruelty.

The book of Jonah reveals the reputation of the inhabitants of the city of Nineveh when Jonah ran in the other direction rather than take God's message to that great city because of their wickedness (Jonah 1:2, 3ff). When Jonah was persuaded, with some help from the great fish, to go and preach to the Ninevites, the people repented of their wickedness and the city was spared God's destruction. Nevertheless, soon after, the city was taken by a coalition of the Medes, Babylonians and Scythians in 612 B.C., and the dominance of the Assyrians upon civilization came to a rather quick end.

Neo-Babylonia

As the Babylonian conquerors rose in control, the Neo-Babylonian period (also known as Neo-Chaldean) came into being. Nebuchadnezzar (605-560) is the Neo-Babylonian king most mentioned in the Bible. Chapters 24 and 25 of II Kings tell how Nebuchadnezzar destroyed Jerusalem and deported hordes of the people of Judah to Babylon. The reason for this deportation of God's people to Babylon is given in II Chronicles 36:5-7.

Basalt "lion of Babylon" stands in the ruins of Babylon.

The prophet Daniel was one of the captives taken to Babylon. We see the height of the glory of Nebuchadnezzar's reign in the book of Daniel, particularly chapters 2,3, and 4. We read of the king's collapse in Daniel 4:28-33, as he is shown dwelling with the beasts of the field, eating grass as an ox.

Persia

In his interpretation of King Nebuchadnezzar's dream, Daniel told the king that his kingdom, likened to the head of gold in an image, would be overtaken by one inferior to his. This was a rule of the countries of Media and Persia, likened to the two arms of the image. Under King Cyrus, the Persians took the lead and established the mighty Persian empire. God had used the Neo-Babylonian King Nebuchadnezzar to take His people into captivity for seventy years as punishment for their continuous worship of idols and disregard for Him (Jeremiah 25:4-11). When the seventy years were completed, God used the Persian King Cyrus to allow His people to return to their land and rebuild Jerusalem (Isaiah 44:27—45:1-6; II Chronicles 36:22,23; and Ezra 1).

The book of Esther gives us a glimpse of the power of Persia and Media and the riches of the kingdom. It also shows the kind of life some of the Jewish people experienced, living under this rule.

Media and Persia occupied the land east of the Tigris and beyond the mountains from Mesopotamia. It is the country of Iran today. The power of Persia was so widespread at the height of the kingdom that if the ancient Greeks, under Alexander the Great, had not conquered it (in fulfillment of Daniel's prophecy in Daniel 2:39), historians point out that our western civilization might be very different today.

Egypt

The first mention of the land of Egypt in the Bible is when Abram journeyed to Egypt because there was a famine in Canaan (Genesis 12:10). This was in the late 2000 B.C., but archaeological discoveries indicate that people lived in this area as far back as 5000 B.C. As in the early history of Babylonia and Assyria, this area was settled after the great Flood by descendants of Noah, his grandson Mizraim going into the Nile River area in the northeastern part of the continent of Africa.

Because there is virtually no rain in this area, the people lived, and still do today, within a few miles of the river. As the Nile overflows its banks every summer—from June to October—the water, rich in silt from deeper into Africa, keeps the area on either side of the river extremely fertile. Although the ancient inhabited area was less in size than the state of Massachusetts, the early kingdoms were strong, rich, and influential. The famous pyramids of Egypt, still standing today, show the great engineering feats these ancient people were capable of performing.

We hear most about Egypt in the book of Exodus, where God called Moses to lead his people out of the slavery they had suffered ever since the family of Jacob was forced to go to Egypt from Canaan for food because of famine in the land, much as their ancestor Abram had done years before (Genesis 42-50).

Quite a bit of traveling took place between Egypt and other countries of the ancient world. We read in Genesis 37:25 that the sons of Jacob sold their younger brother Joseph to a group of Ishmaelites traveling with their camels down to Egypt. Because of the vast Arabian desert, traffic between Egypt and eastern countries like Assyria and Babylon, or Persia, whether for trade or warfare, went through the land of the Israelites.

Israel

This area has had other names well-known to Bible students, the more ancient one being Canaan. God told Moses in choosing him as the leader of His people to take the children of Israel "out of the affliction of Egypt unto the land of the Canaanites . . ." (Exodus 3:16,17). In the book of Numbers God describes to Moses the extent of the land of Canaan, that it "shall fall unto you for an inheritance" (Numbers 34:2). Moses' successor, Joshua, led the people into the land of Canaan, conquering it city by city with the promise from God that "every place that the sole of your foot shall tread upon, that have I given unto you, as I said unto Moses" (Joshua 1:3).

Much later, in the second century A.D., the name

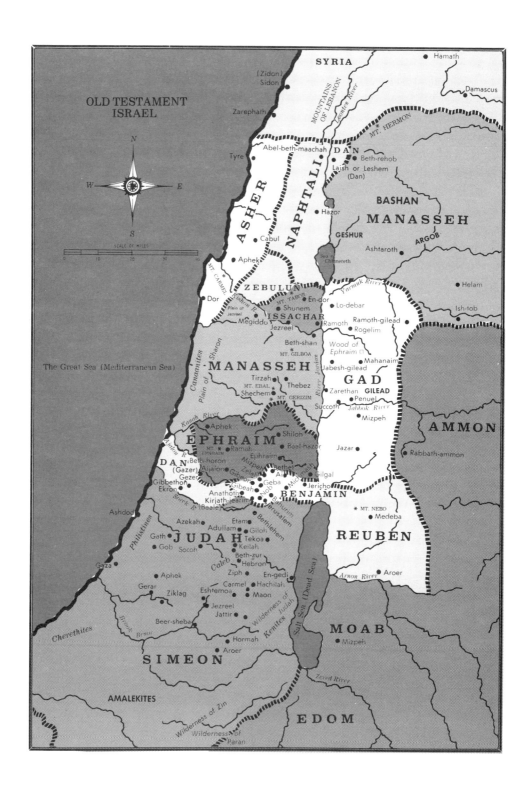

OLD TESTAMENT
ISRAEL

Palestine was put upon the area, first to designate the coastal plain of Phoenicia and eventually to apply to all the area west of the Jordan River. The name "holy land" for this area where the Lord will dwell with His people in the future was used by Zechariah (2:12).

After the Romans, under Titus, destroyed Jerusalem in A.D. 70, the Jews scattered and most of them settled in other lands. Palestine came under several foreign governments; it became an Arab territory, then a Turkish one, and during World War I, the land of Palestine came under the control of Great Britain.

Throughout the changes in forms of government, some Jews continued to live in Palestine. As early as the 1800s Jewish immigrants began to come to Palestine in the hope of establishing once again a Jewish nation and homeland. They faced a discouraging task of restoring a land that had been allowed to go desolate through neglect and misuse, but with dedicated hard work they drained swamps, initiated irrigation systems, dug wells, and planted trees and crops.

By 1948 the Jews declared themselves independent and became the nation of Israel, which was recognized as a nation by the world's powers. Through their industry and education, Israel is today the most advanced country in the Middle East. Repeatedly the small nation has had to defend its independence, and in doing so, obtained more territory, including East Jerusalem, the site of many ancient places called holy by Jews, Christians and Muslims. The Israeli government made these holy sites open to everyone who wishes to visit them.

As we return to our armchair tour, we're docked at Haifa now, nearly 200 miles below Beirut. (Turn your map over to The Holy Land side. You will find Beirut, Lebanon, at about B-4, and Haifa, Israel, at D-3.) We are grateful to know we will stay there a few days, after a stormy night that reminded us of Paul's shipwreck experience in the Mediterranean Sea. We are off to explore Israel now.

The land chosen by God for His people is small. When Bible writers wanted to describe extremes in distance in Canaan, they said "from Dan to Beer-sheba." The throne of David was extended "from Dan even to Beer-sheba" (II Samuel 3:10). Dan (C-5) was at the northern end of

Palestine and Beer-sheba (G-3) at the southern—a distance of about 150 miles altogether. The width of the country is only about 50 miles in the northern section, while at the latitude of Jerusalem (F-4) it is nearer 75 miles.

We will discover in our travels that even this small land is divided into distinct sections by mountains, seas, and climate: The Coastal Plain, along the Mediterranean Sea; the Mountain Region, including the Lebanon Mountains; the Jordan Valley, from the foothills of the Lebanon Mountains to the Red Sea; and the Eastern Plateau, which is Transjordan (east of Jordan).

Touring here in the winter months is not much different from touring in a southern state in the United States in winter, climate-wise. The rainy season during winter lasts about three months and it gets cold enough that a winter coat feels good. Summer, especially on the lower levels, is hot and dry, with temperatures ranging to 120 degrees. Perhaps this heat accounts for some streets with a roof over them, to keep out the hot sun as well as winter rains. You can see why, looking at those meat carcasses hanging uncovered in the markets.

Oddly, Palestine, though stretched along the Great Sea, has few harbors because of its straight coastline. The chief harbor is Haifa, at the foot of Mount Carmel. Modern Tel Aviv has become a close second.

We board buses for a look at the Sea of Galilee, about 30 miles east of Haifa in what is biblically called "Galilee." (Don't let the thoughts of a boat "get to you" after the rough night on the Mediterranean!) This beautiful body of water is about 15 miles long and seven and one half miles wide at its widest part. Notice on your map (D-5) how its shape is somewhat like an inverted pear. It is sometimes called by other names in the Bible: the Sea of Chinnereth (Hebrew for heartshaped), the Lake of Gennesaret after the plain in which it sits, and the Sea of Tiberias after the city on its southwestern shore. In Jesus' time the province in which the sea was located was known as Galilee.

Traveling due east of Haifa and descending to more than 600 feet below the level of the Mediterranean Sea, we will stop in Capernaum first, on the northwest side of the sea. Here we view the ruins that are all that remain of the city that once was home for the Son of God (Matthew

Excavations at Capernaum, near Sea of Galilee, possibly reveal Peter's house.

11:23,24). The main excavation is of an ancient synagogue which has been excavated and partially reconstructed. We see the foundation and floor of large flat stones, columns and carved capitals, and part of a wall that has been restored. One can see in many of the carved stones symbols the Jews used in their religious art—olive branches, the seven-branch candlestick, pomegranates such as the priests wore on the hem of their robes as they ministered in the Tabernacle, and even a representation of the ark of the covenant pictured on a cart with wheels. (The ark customarily was carried by the priests but I Samuel 6:7-16 tells how the Philistines sent the captured ark home to the Israelites on a cart.)

Jesus frequently taught in the synagogue at Capernaum (Mark 1:21; John 6:59). There is evidence that this synagogue was built at a later time, in the second or third century, on the site of the one standing when Jesus taught there. Stones from the earlier synagogue may have been reused in the later building.

"That is Peter's house," our guide tells us, and we see a sign nearby that says so. The "house," of course, is merely

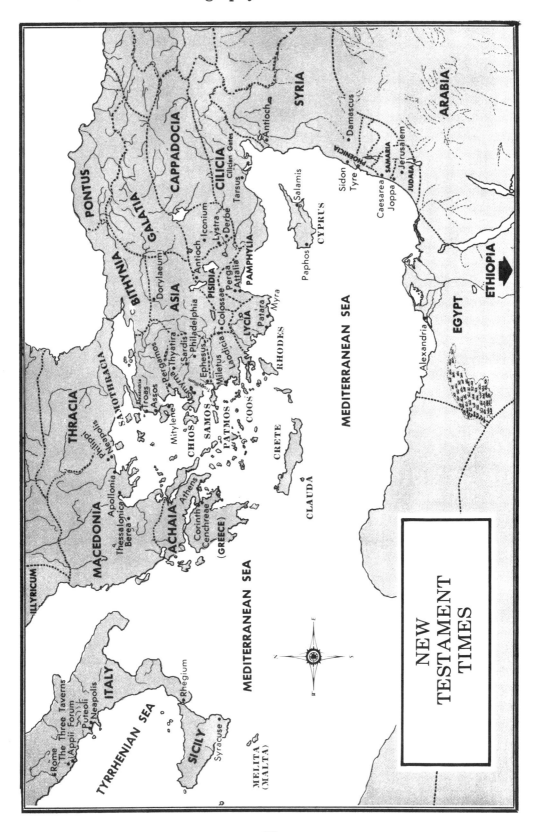

NEW TESTAMENT TIMES

the stone walls outlining the structure and its rooms unearthed by archaeologists. But did Peter ever make his home in Capernaum (John 1:44)? Possibly he settled there after he was married. At least we can see what a house looked like when Capernaum was a city.

The doom Jesus predicted upon the cities around the Sea of Galilee "wherein most of his mighty works were done, because they repented not" (Matthew 11:20) has certainly come to pass. Listen to His words concerning Capernaum: "And thou, Capernaum, which art exalted unto heaven, shalt be brought down to hell: for if the mighty works, which have been done in thee, had been done in Sodom, it would have remained until this day. But I say unto you, That it shall be more tolerable for the land of Sodom in the day of judgment, than for thee" (verses 23,24).

Choose your preferred seat on the motor launch which will carry us across the sea (also called Lake Kinneret on your map). There is a better view from the top deck, and the wind isn't impossibly cold. The guide points out the Mount of Beatitudes. As with many sites, a church has been erected on the site of the spot where Jesus taught His disciples.

Our bus has gone the long way around by land to Tiberias, where we are ready for lunch after the boat ride. The main dish turns out to be "St. Peter's fish" (identified by one guide as bass), which is served complete with head and tail. Rather hard to dismantle a fish which is watching you!

In Galilee, too—as the region around the sea is called—we may stop and see Nazareth and speculate whether yonder hill is one where Jesus may have stood as a boy, looking at the valley below. Not far away, we'll pause at Cana, where Jesus turned the water into wine. Here and there, we pass kibbutzim, the Israeli collective farms, mentioned in another connection later.

Proceeding south the next morning, we go 25 miles southeast of Haifa through Janin; we learn that the Israelis who captured the city during the Six-Day War were kind enough to take care of the livestock of the Jordanians who fled from there until the terms of peace allowed them to return.

Below that city we continue to Sychar to see Jacob's

To see Jacob's Well, one descends through one of the covered doorways shown to the level where the well has been preserved.

Well, where Jesus stopped to rest and told a woman how she could have the Water of Life and she ran to tell the good news to the whole village (John 4). We really comprehend this business of several strata of civilization as we enter a small door and go down steps into the area of the well. Probably the well appears much as it did in Bible times, carved out of black limestone, with rope to lower a bucket, from which one is invited to take a drink of water.

Passing a kibbutz (a collective settlement, usually a large farming area), our guide explains that from age ten all children in a kibbutz have some kind of work to do for an hour every day. All have education for twelve years, after which they, like all young people in Israel, serve a year in the army. The communal living began as a necessity when the Jewish immigrants started resettling Palestine and proved especially successful under the rugged circumstances of those days. Today five percent of the total population of Israel are in kibbutzim, some made up of only American Jews or Jews exclusively of another country; some are settled by youth who wish to identify with their homeland.

Right and left of where we visited Jacob's Well we view places that were only names in the Bible for us before: Mount Gerizim and Mount Ebal, the Mount of Blessing and the Mount of Cursing (Deuteronomy 11:29; Joshua 8:30-35). Between the mountains is Shechem, now known as Nablus, an Arab community.

On the Jericho road, we are reminded not only of the song of that title but of the story Jesus told of the Good Samaritan (Luke 10:30-37). Don't you see how a lonely traveler setting out for that oasis city would be in danger of ambush, as the road goes past hiding places among rocks? We ride down the precipitous way until a sign tells us we are 1300 feet below sea level. We have traveled north east of Jerusalem to about seven miles north of the Dead Sea (near F-4 on the map). Jerusalem is about 2500 feet above sea level, so we do a little mental arithmetic and realize we have descended quite a few hundred feet in the short time since leaving Jerusalem this morning. What a walk these twenty-some miles must have been for Jesus and His disciples as they ascended up to Jerusalem after bringing salvation to the home of Zaccheus in Jericho (Luke 19:1-10,28)!

Beyond Jericho, "local color" takes the form of the "ship of the desert," the camel. We are in wilderness country, where camels are content to eat thorn bushes. At the bottom of the steep brown cliff on which is set the excavated ruins of a house of the Essenes, we see a dry riverbed, called a wadi. Rising on the other side is the cliff in which are the caves of Qumran, the cave which yielded the Dead Sea scrolls a few years ago. You wonder how the boy ever managed to get up there and into the cave.

The hills part and we see the Dead Sea, with surf that rolls like that of an ocean. Curb your desire to taste the mineral-loaded water, as you see some doing. Did you notice how they sputtered? It's even worse—say those who know—to go swimming in those waters and get some water into your nose! No wonder it is called the salt sea in Genesis 14:3. The Jordan River dumps into the Dead Sea, but the body of water has no outlet. Evaporation, which is so heavy that at times it forms dense clouds above the water, leaves a concentration of many chemicals. The surface of the Dead Sea is nearly 1300 feet below the level of the Mediterranean, and the deepest parts are as many feet again deep. The southern end is fourteen feet or less deep, depending upon the season of the year, and it is believed by most scholars that this is the site of Sodom and Gomorrah and the other cities of the plain destroyed in the time of Abraham and Lot (Genesis 19).

Heading west of the northern end of the Dead Sea, we come to "Christmas Town," Bethlehem, labeled on our map "Bayt Lahm" (about F-4). It is called Beth-lehem Ephratah in Micah 5:2, Beth-lehem-judah in I Samuel 17:12 (the home of David's father and his family), Bethlehem of Judea in Matthew 2:1 (recording the birthplace of Jesus), and the city of David in Luke 2:4 and John 7:42. The little town, now inhabited mainly by Arabs, many of whom are Christians, is only about five miles south of Jerusalem. Located in the Judean hills, it is actually at a level higher than the city of Jerusalem.

To visit the "Grotto of the Nativity," one must stoop at the low door and descend stairs in the Bethlehem church.

In Manger Square, we stoop to enter a small door which goes into the Church of the Nativity. What looks like a cellar door inside is opened and we descend into the cave where we see "the Grotto of the Nativity." It is one of the sacred sites chosen by the mother of Constantine in A.D.

320 to commemorate events in the life of Jesus by erecting a church building over them. Whether the silver star inlaid in the marble floor is actually over the place of Jesus' birth, we are moved to contemplate that in this area God's Son became man to be our Saviour.

The "Grotto of the Nativity" has little resemblance to a manger scene.

We hardly realize when we leave Bethlehem and enter Jerusalem to the north, so short seems the stretch between. The Holy City, greatly modernized in its expanded boundaries, was in Bible times bounded by walls. Through the years since David's time, the Old City has actually known several walls indicating different boundaries. The city and its walls were totally destroyed under the Roman attack in A.D. 70. The walls we see today were built, for the most part, in the sixteenth century A.D., under Suleiman the Magnificent while Palestine was under the rule of the Turks. (See "Walled City of Jerusalem" inset on the Holy Land map.) The site of Solomon's Temple (rebuilt by Herod) is now occupied by the Dome of the Rock, a mosque built by the Mohammedans in A.D. 686. The great rocks that form the western foundation of the former Temple site were placed there in Herod's time. This is the only known portion of wall dating to the time of Christ and when the Temple still existed. It is cherished by the Jews as their Wailing Wall, better known today as the Western Wall.

The Dome of the Rock mosque is prominent on the Temple site as one views Jerusalem from the Mount of Olives.

We can take a walk around the walls, if we wish, looking at the towers and many gates, the distance being but two and a half miles. Or, like many tourists do, we may prefer to take a walking tour of Old Jerusalem within the walls. If we enter at the Damascus Gate on the north and wend our way southward to the Zion Gate, the distance would be less than a mile (see the Jerusalem map). We will be enticed by the many shopkeepers along the way urging us into their stalls or bazaars—small shops well stocked with wares all the way from curios and religious mementoes to food and household goods or clothing.

Or, taking a shorter route, bearing to our left, we will visit the ruins of the Pool of Bethesda, where Jesus healed the impotent man. The story is related in John 5. If your courage matches your curiosity, you can crawl around among the ruins and investigate the depths of the pool ruins (originally 80 feet deep, but now mostly filled up with rocks, broken columns and other refuse).

Inside the Old City of Jerusalem, near the St. Stephen's Gate, stand the interesting ruins of the Pool of Bethesda.

Nearby, as mentioned in John 5:2, is the sheep gate in the wall. Since Stephen was stoned to death for his defense of his belief in Christ (Acts 6:9—7:1-60) outside this gate, it is known today as St. Stephen's gate. Let's step through this gate—be careful you don't get run over by that donkey carrying the load of boxes on his back. The view is beautiful from here. Across the Kidron Valley, immediately below, is the Mount of Olives. Down there to the right you can see the tall trees designating the Garden of Gethsemane, where our Lord was praying when Judas led the soldiers to take Him. Raising our gaze toward the top of Mount Olivet, we remember that Acts 1 describes how our risen Saviour ascended upward from this mount and a cloud received Him out of the disciples' sight.

Reentering the city, we soon find ourselves on the Via Dolorosa (the way of sorrow). You may want to follow the "Stations of the Cross" marked along this way, if you watch closely for the signs. These "holy places" (numbered from 1 through 14 on the map) have long been venerated by the Roman Catholic Church as where incidents took place along Jesus' route from Pilate's judgment hall to the cross and the place where He was laid in the sepulcher. The last five numbers mark places within the Church of the Holy Sepulcher itself, making the place of the cross on Calvary and the sepulcher in which His body was laid surprisingly close together.

Most Christians visiting Jerusalem in recent years find Gordon's Calvary, outside the wall and north of the Old City (see map) more fittingly the place where Jesus Christ died. A tomb cut out of solid rock in a garden nearby beautifully coincides with the descriptions given in the Gospels of the place where they laid His body to await His resurrection. It is a beautiful place to visit and to meditate and worship our Lord. We cannot be sure, however, that this place near the hill which looks like the "place of a skull" (the meaning of Golgotha) discovered by the English general Charles Gordon in 1883 is truly where Christ was crucified. We do not need a geographical spot to venerate in order to worship our risen Saviour. We worship the Lord Jesus Christ of the Bible, and He lives in our hearts.

Moving along from one sacred site to another, our directions, distance and time become blurred and weary. Confused travelers say, "I will come again and *stay* in Jerusalem and spend as much time as I wish at each holy spot. I will meditate there about its place in sacred history—His story."

3
Learning From Archaeology

"I Love a Mystery" fans in radio's heyday thrilled to the vicarious experiences of sleuths who solved a variety of mysteries. Men and women who "dig up the past" in the science of archaeology lead equally fascinating lives. They are literally "underground detectives." From their discoveries, they answer questions such as "What race of people hunted animals with this kind of arrow?" "How long ago did people use this particular kind of pottery in their cooking?" "What religion worshiped idols such as *this* one?"

Archaeologists are quick to explain that they are not fortune-hunters, eager to dig up rich treasure to sell to the highest bidder. Instead, their "treasure" may be a seemingly insignificant figurine or a clay pot. But they are excited because that particular kind of clay was used twelve centuries ago by a specific nation. Its discovery is their first clue that they have at last found an important ancient city.

A Christian archaeologist once declared, "We do not need findings in order to prove the Bible is true. We know the Bible is true, if no one ever finds anything about a specific king or city." Nevertheless, there is cause for rejoicing when the pick and spade unearth a clay tablet putting unbelievers to rout.

Actually, a team of archaeologists often rely heavily on the Bible for guidance in their search for ancient cities. Such a team may be composed of specialists in half a dozen areas: anthropology, chemistry, zoology, botany, geology and the Bible. Each has a distinct responsibility in the location, classification, and identification of the finds. (Recommended books on the subject, in Chapter 11, explain in detail the part each plays.)

Mounds (Tells)

In our armchair tour, we discovered that many famous biblical sites must be approached by going down a flight of stairs to a level below the ground. This is because one generation may reclaim a previously inhabited site by simply smoothing out the existing ruins and building on top of them. Debris of the old occupation has mingled with the dust of disintegrated mud houses. Smoothed out, it becomes the next ground level. Because this kind of rebuilding has taken place repeatedly, man-made hills called "mounds" exist. When archaeologists have determined that one of these mounds may be the location of a sought-after city or temple—or whatever— it is labeled by them a "tell." We will explore a few such tells and consider some of the exciting finds.

Detecting which mounds may conceal a long-sought palace or fortress or a city wall is not left to guesswork. A scientific approach may include:

1. A ground survey. Experienced archaeologists can walk over a possible site and observe by the growth of trees and even weeds, whether some stone construction is under the surface, stunting the vegetation.

2. Photographic survey. Instead of tramping over the ground, some teams take aerial views of the land under consideration. They study the enlarged pictures to see whether poor vegetation or sunken land gives them a clue to a possible underground civilization.

3. Interviews. Questioning people who live in the proposed area may provide other clues: Have some of them found unusual objects that belonged to a former civilization? Have they heard stories about events that took place at that site?

4. Metal or moisture detectors. New devices are being used which tell a team whether a certain type of building material lies below the earth's surface.

5. Paper research. If other digging has been done at a given tell, a good archaeologist will find out everything possible through the published reports.

Digging

Probably the clearest analogy to the kind of digging often done at a tell is the construction of a modern superhighway. Bulldozers and blasting cut down through hills, until several layers of earth and rock are visible to those in the cars that whiz by—the bared interior of the earth. Archaeologists may dig a trench through several layers of earth. This allows evaluation of the various strata or levels and avoids waste of time and money that could result from removing the earth one layer at a time.

Digging any kind of hole requires some place to deposit the undesirable or carefully sifted dirt. Careful systems of waste removal must be worked out. Local men and boys are often employed to wheel away barrows of waste material.

Local workers are hired by archaeologists to help move debris from a digging site.

Whodunit?

Archaeologists may be said to operate on the geometric principle that "Things equal to the same thing are equal to each other." Here is how it may work in connection with one means of identification: pottery.

"This pottery material, color and design are peculiar to such-and-such a race of people in 950 B.C. All the pottery in this strata is of this color and design—therefore the people who lived here did so in 950 B.C."

Likewise, "Certain coins were peculiar to a certain nation at a given time. Therefore the people who occupied this strata of ground did so during that period of time."

The discovery of certain funereal practices is likewise applicable: "A specific religious group, during a given era, practiced the burial rites here indicated. Therefore the people who occupied this area were of that civilization."

What's New?

1. *Gamla.* In 1976, archaeologists began to dig at a new site discovered through a survey of the Golan Heights in Syria. It is Gamla, northeast of the Sea of Galilee, not far from Capernaum. The story is as captivating and tragic as that of Masada, where Jewish rebels died by their own hands as their stronghold fell to Rome. In fact Gamla is called "the Masada of the north."

The whole thrilling story is related in the *Biblical Archaeology Review* of January-February 1979. It was detailed by Josephus, first-century historian, from his own firsthand information: he commanded the Palestinians in Gamla's rebellion against Rome, A.D. 67. Like the Masada rebels, the occupants of Gamla made a suicide pact rather than be taken by the Romans.

Surviving this pact by trickery, Josephus and one other Jew surrendered to the Romans. Because he predicted the great future of Vespasian (who became Emperor of Rome two years later), the life of Josephus was spared. His account of the events of Gamla—all in third person—is printed in the BAR.

Like Masada, the site of Gamla is atop a high mountain, surrounded by deep valleys. Parts of the city wall and some houses have been excavated, together with numerous Roman catapult stones, used to destroy Gamla. A large public building, believed possibly to be a synagogue, is considered an important discovery there.

2. *Herodian Jericho.* This is the Jericho of Jesus' time and the site has been under the spade since 1973. A huge swimming pool, significant in historical accounts of the palace, is one of the discoveries. Also excavated are ritual baths, a royal bath and parts of the Herodian palace. Besides the warmed baths, the "cold room" of the area,

called the "Frigidarium," has also been partly restored.

3. *Noah's Ark*. Public interest in one of the earliest Bible accounts has been heightened in recent years by expeditions to Mount Ararat in Turkey. Numbers of books have come out of those efforts, some explorers sure that the ancient ark has indeed been sighted, others equally sure that the structure seen in the ice on the mountain could not be the ark. (See Chapter 7 on slides, for information about those available on this subject.)

4. *Tell Mardikh-Ebla*. Near Aleppo, Syria, about 75 miles north of Damascus, this tell has been the work of a team of Italian archaeologists from the University of Rome since 1968. It is a 140-acre mound, about 50 feet high. The Italians were excited when they found a statue of a king, with an identifying inscription. But in 1974 the tell became of greater significance when they unearthed an archive of 42 clay tablets. Even that discovery paled beside the "jackpot" of 1975: in one place were 1,000 clay tablets and in another, 15,000. The tablets have been of special interest to Bible scholars, partly because of their antiquity. They predate the time of Abraham. Some of

Metal sheeting shades the excavation of a room at the Tell Mardikh site north of Damascus.

those records refer to Bible cities and to names of Bible persons and have refuted critics who had argued that the Bible was a book of fables, saying, "No such towns have been found; no such names were given to people in that area."

Translation of the tablets continues; other valuable facts are being learned from them.

5. *Patriarchal Cities.* BAR (magazine cited in No.1) last year published an account of progress at the excavation of Givat-Sharett, a small city near the Beth Shemesh tell. Listing Bible texts which show that Abraham invariably lived *near* a city, not in it, they have found such a smaller village in Givat-Sharett. It is constructed of ten square blocks of four houses each. Some houses are more elaborate than others. A temple has been unearthed at the top of the hill. Objects of worship have been found within it, including a seven-branch oil lamp and incense burners. Burial caves have yielded clues to the prosperity of the village's former occupants.

Earth dug up on a site is often sieved so small objects are not overlooked.

You can add to your own archaeological experience vicariously by delving deeper into the books and visuals listed in the last chapter of this book.

4
Using Maps and Globes

To the carpenter, a hammer and nails are indispensable tools. To the teacher of Bible geography, maps and globes are equally necessary.

But there are hammers . . . and there are *hammers*. There are nails . . . and *nails*. A tack hammer and small finishing nails do a good job of holding a picture frame together, but the tack hammer would not do much toward sending a tenpenny nail through a two-by-four. There are also maps . . . and there are *maps!* What kind shall we use? What is suitable? Furthermore, where can the suitable ones be found?

Choose the Map for the Purpose

A suitable map for a Sunday School classroom wall is one where names of the chief cities are clearly visible—not just the map. To discover the need, hang on your classroom wall some printed material of the size your proposed map would be. Now, place yourself in the chair of the pupil farthest from that wall. Can you read the print from where you sit? If not, neither can the pupil. The map may be a blur of pretty colors. If so, something larger is indicated.

"But all I have is a small map included in the Teacher's Resource Packet. What can I do?"

There are two options:

You could get the map enlarged. Freehand map drawing is often a project assigned in the public school. Some artistic pupils really enjoy the challenge. If there is an able pupil, by all means increase his interest by asking him to enlarge a map. Said the "Cheerful Cherub" of bygone years:

Some don't get nothin' out of life,
But when their whines begin,
I think I could remind them that
They don't put nothin' in!

The more a pupil can put into the class, the greater his interest will be in the success of that class.

On the other hand, if there is no pupil capable of doing the enlargement, "do it yourself." Not many teachers have the time or the patience to follow the oft-printed instructions for squaring off the map with one-inch squares, and then squaring off the large sheet of paper with bigger squares—and then matching squares and copying the outlines square by square. There is a much easier way, if you have an enlarging projector. Called an "opaque" projector, this teacher's aid is described in Chapter 6, where three different ones are listed. You become an "instant artist" by simply reflecting the enlarged image onto the big sheet of paper, and tracing the reflected outline.

Instead of paper, a window shade from the thrift store or a section of plastic floor covering may be used—the kind florists use on the church aisle for a bride's train to fall on for protection. After a wedding, such a runner is often discarded. Ask for it. One wedding would furnish durable white plastic material enough for a whole set of maps. Chapter 5 on Map Fun has other ideas for its use.

Your second option is to browse through a Christian book shop's map section, or a Christian publisher's catalog until you find just the right size map. Buy it.

Your choice between these options will depend on the time and financial resources available to you or the church.

Some maps are excellent for personal study, but would be utterly worthless on a classroom wall. For private study, you may be happy with a map with names of all the possible towns in a given area, just as you may prefer a road atlas with the names of even the small towns on it. But such an atlas would not be useful for a class geography resource, unless each pupil had one at hand, together with a magnifying glass.

One such small-print, thoroughly cluttered but extremely helpful map is the excellent National Geographic map referred to in Chapter 2, "Lands of the Bible Today," with "The Holy Land" map on the reverse side, 28x40". This map is available from National Geographic Society (see Chapter 11) in both paper and plastic, at $3.00 and $4.00 respectively. They have another good map called "Holy Land Today" at the same price, with biblical and archaeological notes.

Travelers to Bible lands can purchase over there some maps seldom available in Western lands. One such map which has been distributed in the United States is called "Pilgrim's Map of the Holy Land." (A Stateside source is American Mission to the Jews.) The printer is listed as Carpenter's Workshop, Tel Aviv, P.O.B. 3321, Israel. The price is in the neighborhood of $1.00. A gem for clarity of the most notable cities and bodies of water, this map is also rich in background Scriptures and information for Bible students. It does not, however, include much more than Israel, or Palestine.

Another large (19x22"), clear map is available as part of a quarterly package of pictures. The Bible Picture Roll from Union Gospel Press has a beautiful full-color picture for each of twelve lessons in a quarter, plus a map of the unit's study area. These are around $2.50.

A set of clear and colorful 17x22" classroom maps is obtainable from the Nazarene Publishing House. It includes eight maps in full color and ten charts of Bible history and geography—all for $4.50. A teacher may also purchase a miniature set for each pupil for thirty cents.

Irene Ranney's Outline Maps with a few outstanding cities clearly printed may be ordered from Through the Bible Publishers.

Broadman Press has a set of twelve full-color maps, 11x14", listing at $3.50. They also have an outline map set of Paul's Journeys, 18 copies of the same map for pupils to color and use. Order from a Baptist bookstore near you or from the Baptist Book Store in Nashville. From them you may also obtain a set of two children's Bible study maps, 34x22" and 17x14", clearly showing the Bible world.

From Abingdon Press comes a set of clear, uncluttered, colorful maps of the various eras studied in Sunday School. Write for their catalog. These maps are among the most usable, because the names are easy to see in a larger-than-average classroom. (See Chapter 6 on using the Overhead Projector for description of their map transparency sets.)

Picture Maps

Amir's Pictorial Map of Jerusalem is another highly useful study map that comes from the Holy Land itself. The printer is given as Japheth Press, Ltd., 6 Harkevet Street, Tel Aviv, Israel. The detail of this map is clear, showing historical sites and modern Jerusalem. It lists historical sites, monuments and institutions.

In the United States, Friendship Press in New York City is an outstanding source of picture maps of many different areas. A list of their supplies may be ordered from them. The huge map (about two yards long and more than a yard wide) comes ready to be colored, with small pictures to be colored by pupils and pasted on the map. One on Bible lands is listed at $1.25.

Some of the most enchanting geographical materials come from the Wright Studio in Indianapolis. Request their list of materials. In the section under "Middle East," they list a Middle East "Mapkin," which is a map on a napkin. At something like three cents apiece, each pupil could be provided with a colorful map of Bible Lands. Patterns for various Bible people, animals, and trees may also be ordered.

Map Booklets

In addition to their sets of individual maps, Hammond, Inc., has a 48-page *Atlas of Bible Lands*, 9½x12¼" in size, for $3.50. Standard Publishing has a smaller size atlas of sixteen maps plus additional pages of historical information and pictures.

The American Bible Society has a small booklet of eight maps with an index.

Baker's Bible Atlas (Pfeiffer) is another good collection of maps, published by Baker Book House at $5.95. They also have a pocket atlas by the same author at $1.95.

And Then What?

What can you do with a map, besides mount it at the pupil's eye level on the wall? Many boys and girls will never voluntarily go near it. How can you insure at least some knowledge of Bible geography shall rub off on them? The following chapter makes suggestions about ways to use the maps. Additional chapters provide ideas for games and activities to impress knowledge of Bible places.

5
Making Map Study Fun

Unless you are a cartographer, who says maps are fun? The answer is, boys and girls and youth who have taken part in some of the activities described in this chapter—not to mention adults. The trick is in seeing not only the map before your eyes, but in seeing the possibilities of using it to involve pupils in the learning process. It is looking at a map and asking, "Now what can we *do* to impress these names and facts?" That is what this chapter is about—*doing*.

Laminate the Map

For the uninitiated, the big word in the subhead means simply that a map has been given a covering of clear contact paper which can be written upon. Certainly there are other ways to cover the surface of a map, but none so durable. You can take a sheet of "Handiwrap" or "Saran Wrap" or another brand of clear plastic material. If the map is small enough, you can slip it into a large Ziploc storage bag to use for some of these activities, then unzip it and slip it out for filing—the map, not the bag.

Having covered the map, you are ready to let pupils take a grease pencil and trace the travels of a person or a tribe. Since more than one itinerary may be involved over a unit of study, if you wish to trace several different routes and keep them all in view, use different colors of grease pencils.

Right here you will run into complications at your local five-and-dime or office supply store. They just don't have that many calls for different colors of grease pencils. Stores may buy them to put the prices on the bottom of a piece of china or the glass of a picture. But there is a source of four different colors of grease pencils—black, blue, green and red, the set for $1.20. That source is a nationwide school supply house, Beckley-Cardy. Because of the thousands of schools which call upon them for their materials and equipment, this huge supply house can sell almost any item for much less than it can be purchased at a local store, and with a much wider assortment. Listed Number 1 under Catalogs in Chapter 11.

Provided with a grease pencil, a pupil may be called to the map to draw a line to show that Paul went from, say, Troas across the water to Macedonia. In so doing, the person may notice, possibly for the first time, that Paul must have had to go by boat, for they will see a fairly large body of water shown on the map. A second pupil may be allowed to continue the tracing of the itinerary to another point.

If all pupils have a set of maps for seatwork, those may be laminated (with contact paper) and the routes marked in grease pencil so the map can be reused. If the story concerns only one location, let them mark that place with an asterisk or a small sketch of a key object. For instance, at the point where David picked up the five smooth stones from a brook, Elah, they may draw a stone or a slingshot. Since such seatwork would not require much use of a grease pencil, the pencils may be cut in half so all may be provided with one at the same time. It may be wise to collect and store both the map booklets and the pencils at the church.

Picture Map

In the preceding chapter, information was given about picture maps which may be purchased. Small outline maps may easily be made by placing a Bible-size map over a piece of carbon paper and tracing just the outlines onto plain white paper. If a ballpoint pen which is out of ink is used, it will not affect the original map. The outline map can be mounted on the wall or fastened to the bulletin board. Sunday by Sunday, a small picture or object may be placed at the point of the lesson location. The pictures may be the focus for review the following Sunday.

Puzzles

Juniors and young teens can make map puzzles and have them for presession use. They may use Tritex or rubber cement to fasten a map to the flat surface of a styrofoam meat tray. Cut the map into odd shapes.

Floor Map

Using the florist's plastic runner described in Chapter 4, fasten two widths of it together to form a piece large enough to cover a section of open floor area at the front of the classroom. Make a rough freehand enlargement of the map of Palestine on that huge plastic background. Place a black dot at the site of cities and bodies of water referred to in lessons on the life of Christ. Divide the class into two sides (count off by twos to help separate close friends). Alternating sides, ask: "Go and stand on the dot which marks Nazareth," "Put your foot on the Dead Sea," and so on until the dots are covered by standing pupils. Count all those on Side 1 and then all those on Side 2. Those with the most standing are declared winners.

This is a fun game for an outdoor activity, if chalk may be used on an asphalt parking lot.

Link-a-Chain

With maps open, pupils are given the count of ten to find answers. The first player names a Bible place; the next one must name a place which begins with the last letter of the first-named place. As, No. 1 says "Bethlehem" and No. 2 says "Marah," and so on around the class. The process forces pupils to study the map and look at names.

Relief Maps

One Sunday while the class is having a unit study on the Life of Christ, plan a change in lesson scheduling to allow a whole class period to be devoted to preparing a relief map of a clay type mixture. An easy-to-use molding material is made by mixing 3 cups sawdust, ⅔ cup dry wallpaper paste, and 1 cup water. On a corrugated cardboard 16x22" or larger, outline the map with a felt-tip marker. Indicate the bodies of water. Let pupils put the clay on the map and shape it to show the mountains and valleys. Use aluminum foil or mirrors to show the lakes and seas. The following Sunday, when the clay has dried, allow early comers to use water colors to paint the map with different colors for each of the four chief land areas, or each political division. Another pupil may carefully print the names of a few chief cities. Invite parents to see the finished map. Spray it with Clear-Cote plastic to use as a future resource.

For guidance in molding mountain and valley and water areas for your relief map, see page 4 of *Hammond's Atlas of the Bible Lands* (Hammond, Inc.). Smaller but equally efficient for the purpose are Maps 1 and 2, following page 108 in *Baker's Pocket Atlas of the Bible* (Baker Book House).

Flannelgraph Map

Make an outline map on a piece of blue outing flannel (or brushed nylon, velour or felt, since much of flannel no longer has a nap). Let the class cut out the shapes of the political divisions from different colors of similar fabric or velour paper (something which will adhere to the background material) and label them.

The pupils may use the map during presession as a puzzle, or be called on during the teaching period to place a section pertinent to the lesson. Small pictures of key objects may be placed at the city locations where action takes place, too. Pupils may cut such pictures from discarded Sunday School papers and back them with velour or blotting paper.

A similar effect is obtainable by using an enlarged paper map and gluing a small piece of Velcro at the center of geographical sections. Glue Velcro on the sections made by pupils. A tiny square of Velcro may be glued at each city which will be marked with a small picture.

Chalkboard

For a one-lesson use, a map may be outlined on the chalkboard. Pupils may use their Bible maps to find the names of points indicated by dots on the board. They may be given turns printing the names of cities at the proper places, or to indicate the progress of a journey with colored chalk. In this and any map project, use the talents of pupils whenever possible, to insure added interest.

Crossword Tiles

Use a permanent-type marker (such as ballpoint embroidery paint) to print an alphabet letter on each of a few dozen one-inch ceramic tile squares. (Cardboard may be substituted.) During presession, let pupils work by twos and threes on a 16x22'' piece of cardboard, spelling out Bible place names with the tile letters. They may build up a crossword puzzle, by using letters in a previous name as part of another word. As, if HEBRON is spelled out, the R may become the first letter of ROME.

Juniors like a challenge. If several pairs of them are working on this project, it can become a contest to see which can make the most names before time for class to begin. Whenever an alphabet letter is lacking in the tiles provided, they may turn over an unwanted letter and let it be the missing letter.

There's More . . .

Students of all ages except preschoolers may become involved in the use of a most versatile piece of equipment. The Overhead Projector is more than a visual aid for the use of the teacher. It can become a memory aid for students as well, as detailed in the following chapter.

6

Variety with the Overhead Projector

If your church has an overhead projector, its occasional use can add a new dimension of interest in the mastery of Bible places.

Let's call the overhead projector by one of its nicknames, "the electric chalkboard." At once some map-teaching possibilities come to mind, when we remember that pupils like to write on a chalkboard. They become even fonder of writing on a transparency.

Directions for use of this projector and many good ideas are shared by author Anna Sue Darkes in her book *How to Make and Use Overhead Projector Transparencies*, (Moody Press). The book and supplies may be ordered from her company, Faith Venture Visuals, in Lititz, Pennsylvania. See also the listing in Chapter 11 of this company's *Projectable Bible Atlas*. Projectors and supplies are obtainable from a number of publishing houses, among them Beckley-Cardy, identified in Chapter 11.

Materials Needed

Map Transparencies. Abingdon Press has a complete set of six sets of map transparencies, covering all the Bible lands and contemporary Palestine. The complete set lists at $85.00, but may be purchased separately as follows:

Old Testament Palestine. $13.95
New Testament Palestine. 9.95
Contemporary Palestine. 13.95
Old Testament Lands of the Bible. 12.95
New Testament Lands of the Bible. 19.95
Old and New Testament Jerusalem. 19.95

For the teacher who carries a full load of employment, with home and church duties thrown in for good measure, a set of professional quality map transparencies can assure having on hand just the aid needed for any given study. Where individual teachers could not purchase expensive materials for themselves, the church may be able to buy a set for the media center (often the library).

On the other hand, "do it yourself" is no real problem, even to the unartistic, when it comes to making map transparencies. Faith Venture Visuals lists a new, inexpensive kind of plastic for transparencies which sells for $3.95 per 100—making them about four cents a sheet for 8½x11" sheets. Using them, anyone may become an "instant artist." Here's how:

Map Transparency Making

Place the sheet of clear plastic over a map from a Bibleland atlas. Use a transparency marker (see Faith Venture Visuals or Beckley-Cardy listings) and follow the outlines of the map and its divisions with it. It's simpler than making a carbon copy, since you don't have to bear down hard on the point—in fact, you'd better not do so. Trace all the divisions and bodies of water. Make dots at important sites. To allow pupil participation let some of them carefully print the names on the map transparency when they locate them on their own Bible maps, or when they have searched a wall map. When they have seen the enlarged projection of their handwork, they will need no further admonition to "do your best."

For a class of less than ten pupils, let each make an overlay of a specific section of the map. For instance, one may outline the map. A second may add the rivers and lakes; a third may draw and color one division of the country; a fourth may color another area, and so on.

Rearrangement of class schedule may be necessary, to allow completion of the overhead transparency project in one session. Portions of the program omitted may be given extra time the following week or two. Such a change becomes part of the "variety that is the spice of teaching."

Tracing Progress

With the four different colors of grease pencils (Beckley-Cardy), plan ways to involve students in tracing the route taken by a Bible character. For instance, when Jacob flees

60

from the wrath of Esau (Genesis 27), let a pupil begin at Beersheba (level with the bottom of the Dead Sea, midway between the sea and the coast) and draw a line from there to Bethel (Genesis 28:10,19).

The scale of miles is an interesting study at this point. This is a good time to introduce map reading of distances, for it is a fairly straight course from Beersheba to Bethel. How far did Jacob travel? At least fifty miles. Did he travel that far in one day? Did he walk, run, or ride a horse or mule—or what? The Bible does not say more than "He departed." A little speculation would challenge the imaginations of the pupils. Did Jacob think he could travel fast enough on foot? His final destination was Haran, which, according to *Halley's Bible Handbook* (Zondervan), was 400 miles from Jacob's home in Beersheba. In succeeding lessons, pupils may trace his progress on to Haran.

The different colors of grease pencils (all of which are easily wiped off the transparencies) will clearly show the journeys of the Israelites from Egypt to Canaan, or the missionary travels of Paul, or some of the long walks made by Jesus and His disciples. The pencils, of course, can also be used to highlight any city to which you want to call special attention. Pupils may be given opportunity to do the highlighting.

Picture Maps

Flexible vinyl may be purchased in sheets from Faith Venture Visuals at $3.95 for six sheets. One-inch squares may be given to each pupil, together with a transparency pen or pencil. Assign each to draw a specific small object symbolic of an event or place in the day's lesson. Let them cut out the objects (save the scraps) and, at the proper time in the lesson, place the figure on the map transparency on the projector. Use a flannelgraph figure or Sunday School paper illustration as a tracing pattern for human figures to place on the map at the point of their participation in the story.

Puppets

A puppeteer named Connie Champlin has written a booklet explaining how to make and use shadow puppets with the overhead projector. (Address her at 2051 N. 54th Street, Omaha, NE 68104; the booklet is $2.50.) The puppets are made from tagboard taped to a popsicle stick or tongue depressor. This enables them to be moved from place to place. Pupils may talk for the characters, or speech may be taped.

Bible Customs

From Scripture Press, for only $7.95 a set, you may purchase a set of twelve really superior transparencies depicting "Life and Customs of Bible Times." The book also includes twelve duplicating masters for pupils to have copies for classwork involvement. (Milliken Publishing Company makes a hand-roller which turns out these copies, as many as 100 to a master, and costs around $10.00.)

At the same price, Scripture Press also has the same kind of set of transparencies for Biblical Geography, Nations and Peoples of Bible Times, and the Religions of Biblical Times. From them also you may obtain ten different sets of transparencies on subjects pertinent to Bible history. Write for their catalog.

The Nazarene Publishing House has a series of eight transparencies in each of three different sets concerning Bible backgrounds and geography: "How We Got Our Bible," "Maps of the Holy Lands," and "The Spread of Christianity"—each $8.95.

Moody Press has two different sets of transparencies which include Old and New Testament Timelines and are obtainable for $14.95.

7
Projected Visuals of Bible Lands

It used to be true that a Holy Land visitor could not keep up with the requests to show his slides when he got home. Actually, nowadays one need not visit any place farther than the county seat and still be able to present a program of slides from the Holy Land, complete with taped narration.

If the church has a carousel projector with remote forward and reverse controls, a bird's-eye view of a particular section of the Holy Land could be accomplished during opening assembly period. Such a program could introduce a new series of study, involving an area different from the previous series.

Slide Sources

Probably one of the first Christian travelers to share his slides with the public was Dr. Howard C. Estep of the World Prophetic Ministry. In the recent past he offered, in exchange for a gift of something like $15.00, choice of one of fourteen different sets of 40 slides each, including: Israel, Petra, Egypt, Patmos and churches of Revelation, Masada, Jerusalem, Greece, and Babylon. An additional $1.00 brings a taped commentary.

A similar offer comes from Bible Land Slides. They listed a 100-slide set with a written 44-page booklet commentary for $27.95. An additional $5.00 is asked for the 90-minute cassette commentary.

Slides alone are available from other sources which sell slides from all over the world:

1. *Visuals.* This company in Miami, Florida, has slides from many countries. You pay 25 cents per catalog (one country each catalog; minimum order for catalogs is

$2.00). Their listing includes Iran-Iraq, Israel, Jordan, Lebanon, Syria and the Holy Land Lecture Series.

2. *Word of Truth Productions* offers slide programs on a loan basis (freewill offering) for church meetings and Sunday School classes. Their titles are full of rich background material regarding archaeology. Write for a list of these excellent resources. Since their sending the list is a favor, it is a Christian courtesy to enclose postage.

3. *Wolfe Worldwide Films* offers a catalog of thousands of beautiful slides in many lands, for 50 cents. Holy Land areas covered include Israel, Lebanon, Iraq, Holy Land and others. Slides are 50 cents each.

4. *GAF Corporation* will (for 25 cents) send a slide catalog of their thousands of worldwide slides. Many listings are of Holy Land sites. The slides come in a sleeve set of 5 for $1.25.

5. *View Master (GAF)*. From the same address as Number 4, you may order a complete list of another resource often relegated to "children's toys." Not so. The View Master is a valuable little piece of equipment for sharing 3-D pictures of the Holy Land and other Bible-related subjects. Thirteen subjects on their list would provide some Bible background—at a current price of $1.80 for each packet of 21 different pictures. The viewer itself is only $3.00. However, it is possible to obtain from GAF a small projector (30-watt) for around $10.00, which will enlarge the pictures to 18 inches. A 100-watt projector for around $20 will show a 30-inch-wide picture. Ordering information is given on the list of available views.

Filmstrip Sources

Filmstrip projectors come in a wide variety of sizes and prices. Chances are that inquiry at your regular Christian supply house will enable you to locate the kind that fits your need and budget.

1. *Prima.* Some Christian publishers (David C. Cook for one) list the products of Prima (a division of Hudson Photographic Industries, Inc., Irvington-on-Hudson, NY 10533). Cook's 1979 Catalog lists Prima's $40.00 filmstrip viewer, which is self-contained, needing no screen, and shows a 4x5" picture. They also show Prima's viewer for 2x2"slides, which has a 5x5" screen and sells for $55.00.

Do-it-yourself filmstrips can be made by the class members with the aid of "U-film" kits from Prima which come with a 25-foot roll of film and 12 colored pencils and other aids and an instruction book for $16.00. If you already have pencils for overhead projector use, the film alone is $7.00 for the 25-foot roll. They have another kit for slide-making also, at the same price.

2. *Nazarene Publishing House.* This company has a series of twelve filmstrips, with manuals, for Sunday School teachers. One of these, on maps and globes, is ordered with #VA6129, for $5.75. Other subjects are the same price.

This publisher also lists a set of two filmstrips and a record ($19.35 total) on "Everyday Life in Palestine," and "Shepherd Life in Palestine." Another set of four filmstrips on "The Land of Jesus" is $50.00 and includes "The Land of Jesus' Birth," "Land of Jesus' Boyhood," "The Land of Jesus' Early Ministry," and "The Land of Jesus' Later Ministry."

3. *Scripture Press.* The Junior Plug-in, a filmstrip-cassette tape combination, comes from Scripture Press on the subject "A Designed Land for a Chosen People." The 50 frames allow material for two different sessions with good background. Cost, only $7.95.

4. *Moody Press.* Moody Science Filmstrips are beautiful combinations of photography and art, presenting four sets of Bible backgrounds filmstrips, with four strips in a set, at $34.00. Filmstrips separately with cassette narration are $11.95. Send to Moody Press for a complete listing and description of the sixteen strips.

5. *Broadman Press.* A 40-frame filmstrip with a manual and cassette tape, "The Land Where Jesus Lived," for $10.00, is a good teaching aid from Broadman.

6. *Word of Truth A-V Ministry.* This company has a filmstrip entitled "The Search for Noah's Ark," available on a freewill offering basis for churches. Good background material.

Opaque (Enlarging) Projector

A church can invest anywhere from $10.00 to more than $200 for an opaque projector, to enlarge small pictures and project them on a screen.

1. *Prima.* Prima's version, also listed by David C. Cook, is $9.95.

2. *Standard Publishing.* Standard has a similar product for $10.95.

3. *Balda Art Service.* Balda handles a more effective, larger version that enlarges more clearly, with larger pictures. A teacher may use a picture that is postcard size or smaller, colored or black-and-white, and project it for the view of a class of 50. This projector sells in the neighborhood of $60.00. No recent listing was available.

4. *Gospel Services.* The Teach-o-Scope, from Gospel Services, Inc., in Houston, Texas, is about the same price and will do the same job.

With a project like the above, you could obtain two copies each of small illustrated booklets and thus use pictures from both sides of a page. Paste them in sequence on a strip of paper the width of the "feed" area, and make up your own filmstrips to illustrate the sequence of a lesson or story. Pupils may be involved in illustrating the lesson, either by selecting and pasting the pictures on the strip, or by drawing a series of pictures on the strip.

If the church has no projector like this, of course, flat pictures are published by most curriculum suppliers to go with the lessons. Some of those will be described in the next chapter.

8
Pictures, Charts and Posters

If you have been giving your class a steady diet of overhead projection or filmstrips, you have already discovered the worst method of teaching: the one that is used all the time. Although you may have several kinds of projectors and an unlimited budget for supplies for each, you will find that eventually a class's reception to projected visuals will become less than enthusiastic. Having lived from coast to coast, in a variety of wage brackets, the author has observed response of pupils to the many methods presented in her book *Successful Teaching Ideas* (listed in Chapter 11). Actually, what is highly successful in one situation will hardly call for raised eyebrows in another. In Washington, D.C., for instance, announcement of a forthcoming filmstrip was received without a murmur; whereas, in a country church, where schools were short of funds for expensive equipment, a filmstrip was a novelty. There was a "Goody! Goody!" kind of reception to the announcement.

So, regardless of the availability of expensive equipment, it will be all the more appreciated if it occasionally goes on vacation while some of its lowly cousins take over.

Pictures

The "social studies" (polite name for geography) of any culture includes not only knowledge of rivers, lakes, mountains and rainfall, it also includes information about the customs (and costumes, if you please) of the people who live in the area. Filmstrips have already been named which supply this background, but not everybody will have filmstrips. Everyone can find some pictures to show what the city of Jerusalem looks like, how a shepherd's robe looks, and how dry the Qumran Cave area is. There are many sources of pictures today, for even *Reader's*

Digest features color illustrations of articles and ads.

We will here omit mention of book and magazine sources of pictures, for they are worthy of more lengthy treatment in a separate chapter. Other sources of pictures include:

1. *Publishers.* Denominational and other curriculum publishers are a source of pictures. Incomprehensible as it may seem, some teachers in smaller churches are not even aware that their publishing house has teaching pictures and other teaching aids to go with every quarter's Sunday School lessons. Such publishers have long been aware (as long as this author has been in Sunday School, which is almost a lifetime) that one picture is worth a thousand words—especially when it comes to describing a land and people the audience has never seen. I still have in my files some pictures from Sunday School papers received as a child in the Primary Department. My newspaper-editor father once bound them together in a book for me.

The pictures may be as large as those described on the Bible Picture Roll, Chapter 4. They may be as small as the picture story cards which Union Gospel Press publishes to match that large chart. In between, there are picture sets 17x24", 9x12", and so on. Most take-home papers have in them a copy of the day's teaching picture.

These pictures are not merely the product of the artist's imagination, and of course there were no cameras in Bible days. While some imagination was required, certainly, it was fed by careful research of the customs and people of the specific place being illustrated. When a picture shows a waterpot of a certain shape, a lamp of a unique kind, be assured the articles were not there merely to add color. In Bible times, the people in the home used that particular article. Hence it is included. Yet how many times a picture is mounted on the wall, or picked up and held for two seconds and nobody has time or inclination to analyze anything about it.

Large teaching pictures afford opportunity for class study, even for preschoolers. Ask, Who can find a dress that is different from the kind of dress your mother wears? Are the men wearing clothes like your daddy or uncle wears? Such questions stimulate the thinking of little ones. Call for careful examination of other details and discuss them, as such study is used on up into the Adult

Department.

Oh—someone says—do you use pictures with adults? Assuredly. Who is it that stays up to watch TV after the kids are in bed? Adults like to learn the easy way and the clear way, by *seeing* as well as hearing about people. Many present-day senior citizens were once pupils in a Sunday School that never furnished take-home picture cards or teaching pictures. They graduated into adult classes with no visual aids—and their concept of Bible customs needs clarifying as much as that of a kindergartner.

If you are in a struggling new church, with no funds for teaching pictures, perhaps you know a friend in a large church which is so affluent that their extra Sunday School papers are thrown on a shelf in a heap every Sunday—until cleanup day. Ask your friend to tell you when to come by and pick up a stack.

2. *Calendars.* Religious art calendars display beautiful Bible pictures year round—and then may simply be discarded as another outdated calendar. Request friends to save them for you, even more than one. Hold onto those numbered squares with Bible verses, too. You will find a use for them in review games.

3. *Greeting Cards.* Christmas and Easter cards, particularly, often feature beautiful art. The small pictures may be used in a variety of ways, besides in slides for the opaque projector described in Chapter 7. Some ways to use pictures are given in the next section of this chapter.

4. *Giant Photos.* The price list of this company in Rockford, Illinois shows miniature pictures of more than 200 different pieces of beautiful art. The 16x20" pictures are 50 cents each and the 8x10" ones are only a quarter. Many of the subjects are religious in theme. Others have beautiful scenes which illustrate the Creation theme. When the listing becomes outdated, the miniature pictures themselves may be used as part of an opaque projector slide set.

Using Smaller Pictures

Story Wheel. Use two poster board circles of the same size, cutting a wedge (pie shaped) in the top one, large enough to frame the pictures below. Cut off the point an inch before the center of the circle. Fasten the two circles together in the middle with a paper fastener. Paste around the bottom circle a series of pictures illustrating the people and customs of an area being studied. For instance, a series of pictures about the Sea of Galilee region could be: The sea, a Bedouin tent, a fisherman mending nets, a close-up of the kind of fish he would catch, and a view of the land area near the sea. There are other scenes which would be equally useful. The choice may depend on the availability of specific pictures.

Flip Chart. A stenographer's notebook with spiral back makes an excellent lap-size flip chart which may be used with a sequence of small pictures, in the same way the story wheel is used. Paste the small pictures onto the pages in the notebook on one side of a page only for a series for one story. The book will serve for several stories. When the book is full, turn it over and paste pictures in a series on one side only. (See Eleanor Doan's *Visual Aid Encyclopedia* (Regal), pages 40-41, for ways to make a small flip chart and also the stand for a large flip chart.)

Picture Cubes. Now you have a use for those half-gallon (or even quart) milk cartons you have been saving. Square off the bottom section, so that each side is the size of the bottom. Allow the same length above the necessary length, so those flaps may be bent across the open space at top and taped down firmly. Cover the outside of the cube with contact paper, construction paper or wallpaper (ask a paint store for an outdated wallpaper book). Paste on each of the six sides of the cube a picture representing some phase of the land, customs or clothing of the area under consideration. Let older pupils participate in making the cube and in displaying and explaining the pictures. For permanence and durability, cover each side with clear contact paper. A continuous strip for the four consecutive sections will prevent little fingers from getting a grip and tearing it off.

Dioramas. Cut off one side of a square box, and the top and bottom flaps. Paint the inside of the three remaining sides to represent the blue sky and the rolling hills of the Holy Land—green for a springtime scene and brown for summer. Make stand-up people and animals and household articles and place these in the foreground of the diorama. (Doan's book, referred to above, pages 46-47, gives several ways to make figures that will stand up.)

Movie or TV Roll. For full description and picture of this box device, see the author's book *Successful Teaching Ideas,* page 23. Summarized, this is a box (perhaps two feet square or larger) from which one side has been cut out, leaving a 1½-inch frame. This opening is the viewing area. Dowel sticks are inserted top and bottom behind this viewing area. A roll of paper a half-inch wider than the viewing area is taped at each end to the dowel sticks, to allow the roll to be turned, to show the pictures. Pupils can prepare the scroll for the "movie" by pasting or drawing the pictures for it; they can also be responsible for turning the pictures and explaining their own.

Posters

Posters, like bulletin boards, can provide quiet background "atmosphere" just by being there.

Three-D. On a background painted or pasted on a 10x14" piece of poster board, attach trees, people, houses and animal figures by an accordion-folded strip of paper. The moving figures will give a Three-D effect.

Illustrated Text. Print a verse describing a Bible event and illustrate it with a picture showing the event.

Rebus Story. Print an abbreviated version of the Bible story, substituting pictures of people and places and animals mentioned.

Activities such as the foregoing chapters have suggested are means to encourage concentration in learning names and facts. The games explained in the next chapter will afford drill disguised as fun, to impress the facts learned.

9
Games to Help Learning

Visual aids of the foregoing chapters assure that pupils have a 50-50 chance of remembering the geographical facts of a given lesson. Through the review games here, we are allowing opportunity to deepen those impressions to 70 percent memory retention of what *they say* and 90 percent of what *they do*. Some games will provide both factors. The list here is by no means exhaustive. The chapter on books and magazines gives sources which will add regularly to the list.

Tic-Tac-Toe. Instead of using a chart with nine blanks to fill in with X or O, use two filled-in charts for a relay race.

Pojap	Yert	Acna
Deen	Robhen	~~Hetbet~~ Bethel
Maarias	Chojier	Pyget

(Across: Joppa, Tyre, Cana, Eden, Hebron, Bethel, Samaria, Jericho, Egypt.)

Make the charts identical with the same nine scrambled Bible place names on each. Pupils are divided into two teams. They line up as for any relay race. The first player on each side, chalk in hand, goes to the board and unscrambles one name and rewrites it correctly under the scrambled letters. He then rushes back to his team and gives the chalk to the next in line, who repeats the performance, correcting another scrambled word—and so on until all nine squares are completed. If there are not as many as nine players for each team, the first player takes a second turn, and then the second—until the nine squares are done.

Grab Bag. There are several ways to use this old favorite with Bible place names.

1. Questions. On strips of paper write questions which must be answered by the name of a Bible place. For instance, In what sea were Peter and John fishing when they were called by Jesus? or, Where did Mary and Martha live?

2. Answers. On strips of paper put the names of Bible places, rivers, seas, and so on. Pupils answer by telling an event that happened there.

3. People. On pieces of paper, put the names of Bible characters. As the name is drawn out of the bag, the pupil must state a Bible place associated with that character.

For any one of these variations, the game may be played by passing the bag around the class as long as music plays (tape, record, or piano). When the music stops, the holder of the bag draws out one slip of paper and answers the question. The bag then goes to the next pupil and continues to circulate.

The bag may simply be handed to each pupil in turn as two teams line up facing each other as for a spelldown. If a pupil cannot answer the question, he sits down. The team with the most standing at the end is declared the winner.

Blind Man. This is especially appropriate at a time when a lesson story concerns the healing of one of the blind men. Let a "blind man" (or girl—blindfolded) sit in a chair in the center of a circle. That one is given a box of small Holy Land objects to identify, before the count of ten. Only the teacher knows what is in the box. The teacher writes down the total number of objects identified by the "blind man" and another player is given a turn at being blindfolded. Let two pupils from each side represent their teams. The team with the most correct guesses wins.

Matching. This is a good aid to learning.

For pupils who can read, put two columns on a piece of newsprint or the chalkboard—one of Bible people and the other of Bible places. Let pupils, one at a time, come to the board and match one person with one place by drawing a line between them.

Give each pupil a paper with the two columns typed on it. Let every pupil match all the names and places.

Non-readers may play the game by placing flannel-backed pictures on a flannel map at the proper place.

Scavenger Hunt. Hide about the classroom small articles (or replicas) associated with a recent unit of study. Divide the class into two teams. Give an identical list to the leader of each and let the teams see who can find the most objects on the list in a three-minute period—or whatever time is available for the game.

Where Am I? The book by this name (Moody Press) has clues about Bible places. A teacher may select the rhyming clues that pertain to recent lessons and use them in review of place names, in spelldown or grab bag fashion.

Moving the Mountains. Mountain names are scrambled and listed, together with a clue in the form of a person associated with them. Two teams may have a relay race in unscrambling them, or the two sides may alternate in doing so. The following names and clues (with answers in parentheses) are listed here:

1. TARARA—Noah's Ark (Ararat)
2. ELM CAR—Elijah's altars (Carmel)
3. IDL AGE—Jacob and Laban (Gilead)
4. BE HOR—Burning Bush (Horeb)
5. HAM ROI—Solomon's Temple (Moriah)
6. I SIN A—Ten Commandments (Sinai)
7. RATBO—Barak's camp (Tabor)
8. RISE—Moses (Seir)
9. NIZO—David's palace (Zion)
10. BIG OLA—Saul's death (Gilboa)
11. LAN BONE—Hiram's forests (Lebanon)
12. IG MIZER—Samaritan temple (Gerizim)
13. NAB ASH—Wild cattle (Bashan)
14. LITVOE—The ascension (Olivet)
15. MOR HEN—Transfiguration (Hermon)
16. CRY VALA—The crucifixion (Calvary)
17. AH PIGS—Balaam's seven altars (Pisgah)

True-False. Put a list of statements on the chalkboard, numbered; or make a list for each pupil to do as seatwork. Let them draw a circle around the number of the statement which is incorrect. The following ten are examples. A teacher may prefer to make up a list which pertains especially to a specific unit of study.

1. Palestine is at the western end of the Mediterranean.
2. At the Red Sea many of the Hebrews were drowned.
3. Jesus fed the 5,000 in the town of Cana.
4. Elisha conducted a contest on Mount Carmel.
5. Bethlehem was called the City of David.
6. The disciples were first called Christians in Antioch.
7. Mount Nebo is where Moses died.
8. The Christian Church began in Jerusalem.
9. John was exiled to a prison in Rome.
10. The Jordan is the longest river in Palestine.

(In the above list, the following numbers should be circled as false: 1,2,3,4,9.)

Bible Objects. Provide each pupil with a list of the following multiple-choice questions, or read them aloud and ask each to write *a, b,* or *c.*

1. If you had an EPHOD—would you put it in a cage, take it to church, or plant it in your garden? (b)
2. If you had a FIRKIN—would you fill it with water, sleep on it, or feed it to the dog? (a)
3. If you had a TALENT—would you put it in the bank, eat it, or play a tune on it? (a)
4. If you had a COVENANT—would you sell it, kill it, or try to keep it carefully? (c)
5. If you had a SHEKEL—would you give it to the zoo, chop it down, or buy some fruit with it? (c)
6. If you had a DULCIMER—would you use it for a cane, put the baby in it, or play a hymn on it? (c)
7. If you had a MANTLE—would you cook it for dinner, read it, or give it to a beggar who was

cold? (c)

8. If you had a EWE—would you wear it around your neck, put it in the missionary offering, or give it to a shepherd? (c)

9. If you had a SCROLL—would you milk it, put it in a library, or use it for a blanket? (b)

10. If you had some KINE—would you put them in a pasture, buy a cage for them, or hang them on your Christmas tree? (a)

Bible Occupations. Give a list of references to each of four teams (count off by fours). See which team can first complete identifying the Bible-time occupation named in each. Suggested references include:

Isaiah 64:8	I Kings 9:27
Genesis 50:3	Acts 19:24
Malachi 2:7	2 Kings 12:12
Exodus 2:7	Genesis 4:2
Revelation 18:22	Judges 6:11
Jeremiah 22:14	2 Chronicles 35:23

Household Articles. Give a list of references to each of four teams, as above. See which team can first identify the household articles named in them.

Genesis 44:12	Amos 6:4
Proverbs 7:16	John 4:28
2 Kings 4:10	Exodus 26:1,2
Mark 14:20	Hebrews 10:13
Ecclesiastes 12:6	Jeremiah 52:19

Bible Birds. As for the two preceding games, list references naming birds. Ask the teams to see which can first identify all of them. Suggested references are:

Matthew 3:16	Genesis 8:7,8	John 18:27
I Kings 17:6	Psalm 84:3	Luke 13:34
Numbers 11:31	Job 39:13,14	Psalm 102:6
Psalm 104:17	Isaiah 34:14	Isaiah 40:31

Bible Food. Play this game as for the preceding ones with a list of references to each of several teams. References may include:

Exodus 27:20	I Kings 17:12	Galatians 5:9
Hosea 7:8	Job 6:6	Exodus 29:2

Genesis 18:8   Numbers 11:5   Matthew 13:31

Rhyming Places. Rhymes about Bible places may be used instead of questions in a review game such as a spelldown or grab bag. An example is:

Seven times they marched around the town,
And lo! the walls came tumbling down.

That verse is from *1000 Bible Questions in Rhymes, Puzzles, Quizzes and Games,* which has a list of these rhymes on page 9. (The book may be obtained from a Christian book store or from the publisher, Baker Book House.)

Spin the Bottle. Using a plastic detergent bottle, let teams take turns spinning the bottle. The one to whom it points must answer a question about a Bible place.

Bible Alphabet. Hold up cards with a letter of the alphabet on. By the count of 10, players must call out the name of a place beginning with that letter. The first to do so, gets to hold the card. The holder of the most cards at the end of the game wins.

Five Questions. One player leaves the room. The others choose the name of a Bible city, mountain or body of water. When the player returns he asks questions of the other players, one by one, such as: Is it a river? Is it the river where Jesus was baptized? After the place is guessed, he chooses another player to take his place.

Commercially published games. See your Christian bookstore or catalog.

To further help pupils *do* something to assure 90 percent memory retention, the next chapters give ideas for projects the class can do as a group, including simple drama or role play.

10
Projects to Teach Bible Customs

A project is an activity in which the whole class may participate as a class or as individuals. By so doing, they are reinforcing facts or truth. In this chapter, we will be largely concerned with the facts of biblical customs and/or costumes. The difficulty of the project and the amount of time to be spent on it will vary with the ages and abilities of the class members. It will also vary according to whether the project is started "from scratch" or whether it is made from "pre-fab" materials, if it involves handcrafts.

There are distinct advantages to making the whole project an original creation. Doing it yourself gives opportunity for pupils with original ideas to use them. Their pleasure in accomplishment will be greater when an idea they put forth is adopted and used successfully. We will consider first some projects which can be made from materials easily obtainable.

Palestinian House

Pupils hear with what they *are*—and so do teachers. Say "house" and they envision a structure with which they are familiar: ranch style, gabled, or whatever. Few would think "square and stucco," as the majority of Holy Land dwellings would have been in the time of Christ.

An easy working model for the class may be almost an "instant house," made from a small-size square corrugated carton. Cut off the flaps and turn the box upside down. Cut a two-inch-wide strip off each discarded flap. Glue that strip along the edge of the roof of the house (the bottom of the inverted box) as the protective rail to protect family members from falling off the roof.

Cut out a door (about 2x3", cutting on three sides so the remaining side can be folded back as a hinge to allow it to open and shut). Cut out a small window or two.

Accordion-fold a one-inch-wide strip of heavy brown construction paper, about ten inches long; bend down flaps at the left edge and glue the steps to the house with those flaps. The brown should match the box, if possible.

You may wish to use the box without further painting, unless it is adorned with much printing. The class may add a touch of realism by spraying on a coat of glue and splashing the sides of the house with sand. A thin mixture of molding plaster is another way to coat the outside of the house for an adobe effect.

Your class may like to show the interior of a Palestinian house. This may be done by opening three sides of the roof, leaving the fourth side as a hinge to open it and let the class see inside. Or, instead, one side of the house may be cut away or hinged, to allow the inside to show.

Mexican pottery clay may be purchased from hobby stores or school supply houses (as Beckley-Cardy). Let the class make bowls, waterpots, and lamps which are typical of biblical culture.

Individual class members may make their own houses or a group of houses for a Palestinian village by using a square piece of construction paper. Fold the paper in half in either direction and then fold it in half again the same way. Open it and fold in the opposite direction, twice, as before. The result will be sixteen squares. One square from each end, make a cut two squares long. Bend the flaps over and paste, to form a boxlike structure. Turn the box upside down and add the guard railing, stairs, and windows, as for the larger house.

Tents

Not all Israelites lived in houses then—nor do they now. Some still live in tents. A simple form of tent may be made from a 5x9" piece of construction paper. Fold it in half the short way, so you have two halves 4½ inches long. Open flat and fold each end in a third of the way toward the center. Open and flatten the paper and color the outside with alternating stripes of brown and orange. Crease it again lightly in the center and at the small folds at the edge, so the tent stands alone. It can be used in a sandbox, a diorama scene, or a village model.

Well

Use a small-size tuna fish can. Cover the outside with gray construction paper on which you have marked outlines of stones with a felt-tip pen. Again, you may find contact paper with a "stone" finish.

Tower

Cover an oatmeal box with the stone-finish contact paper or gray construction paper marked as stones. The class may wish to spread or spray glue over one section at a time and actually cover the outside with small pebbles. Finding such pebbles may become the purpose of a class outing to a river or seashore.

Tabernacle

You can make your own model of the tabernacle and the Israelite tents which were set up in the surrounding area. Directions are given for doing this with index cards, in Doan's *Visual Aid Encyclopedia.* Another model, using grocery bags, is described in this author's own book *What's in the Bag?* (See listing in Chapter 11.)

Scrapbooks

An older age-group class may make scrapbooks as a teaching aid for younger children or for a missionary. Younger classes may make them as part of their study, to take home and keep. They can even make the blank-page book for the purpose by using loose-leaf pages of construction paper and binding them into a theme binder. Or they may use handmade covers of lightweight cardboard covered with wallpaper. (See a paint store for discarded, out-of-date wallpaper sample books.) Punch two holes at one edge and lace together with yarn or ribbon.

Encourage map-making, as well as cutting out and pasting in pictures of Bible people and home life. Pupils may be given opportunity to draw items from a pattern in a Bible dictionary.

People

A variety of bases may be used in making people and

animal figures for tabletop or sandbox models.

Chenille-wire figures are easily made by bending one ten-inch wire in half and twisting it to leave a circle at the center for the head. Twist a four-inch piece around the "neck" to form the arms. In a similar way, arms may be added at the neck of a two-pronged clothespin with a round head.

Another "person" figure is made by adding a small styrofoam ball at the top of a thread cone from a sewing factory. Wind a piece of chenille wire around the neck of this figure to form arms.

Dress the figures by folding in half a three-to-six-inch-wide piece of material which reaches to the feet of the figure when folded. At the fold, cut a tiny hole for the neck, but make a one-inch slit down the front so it can be slipped over the head. Use a piece of yarn to tie as a belt at the center, to fasten the garment together. No sewing is necessary.

Paste a face over the chenille-wire circle and add a triangle of cloth for a headdress. Add felt eyes, nose and mouth to the styrofoam head of the cone doll. Use felt-tip pens of different colors to make the features of a clothespin doll.

The figures may be used in a sandbox scene, diorama, or Palestinian village. Stand clothespin figures in a round base of clay.

Animals

Patterns may be found in coloring books. Trace the animal onto a folded piece of paper, with the fold at the top of the animal's back. Cut out except for a strip of the fold, so the animal may be made to stand.

Prefab Models

Study publishers' catalogs to find some of the many excellent prepared models for quick assembly and use. Some come perforated to punch out.

David C. Cook and the Nazarene Publishing House both list a Bible Times Village which includes a synagogue as well as five houses and twelve groups of people. The book adds descriptions of the houses and furnishings and explains customs.

They also have a tabernacle model which comes die-cut and includes the outer fence and the furnishings as well as the figure of a priest.

Field Trips

If your class is in a city where there is a museum, the class might plan a group trip to see the religious art. School groups travel long distances to get to Washington, D.C. to visit the Smithsonian Institution and the National Art Gallery. It could be a memorable experience to take such a trip as a class and later compare impressions of famous art, showing facts about Bible customs seldom pictured in Sunday School materials.

Drama

Instead of a series of twelve lessons in a sit-down-and-listen situation, one Sunday School department spent the three months preparing for a drama on the life of Abraham.

To do this, they had to study the Bible carefully and learn all they could about the customs of the people. They had to research books which gave them insights into customs mentioned in the Bible. They had to study maps and determine the kind of land over which Abraham would travel, the climatic conditions he would encounter. They had to learn what kind of clothing Abraham and his family and servants would wear.

The class members planned their own speeches and scene sequences. The end of the project was an outdoor presentation of one of the most memorable studies the class ever undertook. Not all classes will want to devote an entire quarter to a drama project but it could be a good idea for Vacation Bible School or a camp project.

A one-act play would provide a challenge for several weeks. Write to Baker's Plays, and ask for their *Catalog of Plays for Church Use.* They offer a wide variety, from monologues to three-act plays and pageants with many characters. Baker's Plays also has several good books to guide a class in planning costumes and scenery. One is called *Costuming the Biblical Play,* by Lucy Barton, listing at $3.00.

Travel Folders

An Illinois teacher reviewed and impressed Bible geography by planning a "travel folder" for them to complete. She gave the mimeographed folders to the pupils one week and allowed them to take them home and fill in the blank places she had left. The folder read like a typical brochure describing a Holy Land itinerary, with names of places omitted where the description was clear. Here are a few samples from the folder:

"Each year thousands of pilgrims travel to the Holy Land (now called _____). Almost all of them visit the place where Jesus died, the city of _____. There you see the _____, the street where Jesus carried His cross.

"You will also want to visit in the _____ part of the Holy Land, where Jesus lived for many years and where He worked many miracles—_____."

This type folder could be prepared for a study on a different part of the land, including areas visited by Paul, or traveled by Abraham, and so on.

Interviews

The "talk show" interview technique can be effectively used to present geographical facts and customs, by having a reporter question a Bible character about those facts.

Monologues

Personification requires only a single Bible person, attired with at least a *keffiyeh* (headdress), but not necessarily a robe over his western dress. This person may tell (as his own experience) what happened to him, or report what he *saw* and *heard* in the life of a Bible character at a place where he was a bystander. *The Book of Witnesses,* by Kossoff, has excellent examples of this approach. This comes from Warner Books for $1.25.

For the teacher who has too many responsibilities to think up ideas or work them out from scratch, the following chapter will provide knowledge of sources of help.

11
Sources of Material and Helps

This is not a Bibliography; it is rather a listing of sources of help. Here are mini-reviews of some of the best available literature to help you know the land of the Bible and how to teach what you know.

Catalogs

You have already read in this book—as well as others I have written—that among the first on a teacher's book list should be *Catalogs*. Sears Roebuck probably started the trend back in the Gay Nineties with their pictorial "wishbook." (If you want a real dose of nostalgia, get a copy of a reprint of their Fall 1900 Catalog, which is about $3.50. You will drool over the luxurious furnishings their customers could buy for less than $40 a set—or clothing of the finest kind for less than $10.00.) Some of today's catalog compilers have imagination, too. Colorful pictures and descriptions make a sales pitch for their products. Some, on the other hand, are mere blase lists. But all of them will yield information about materials and books available in a specific area of teaching.

Most Christian publishing houses will send a catalog upon request. They want you to know what they have. When you get the requested catalog, do yourself a favor: Read it! Certainly not word for word through all subjects of no interest to you, but read carefully in your area of interest as though searching for treasure. It may turn out to be just that to you.

The following are some catalogs you should get and know. If some of them differ in doctrine from your church, their methods materials are still worth using.

Beckley-Cardy. This fantastic school supply house has six different outlets for fast service all over the United States. Write their central office in Chicago and they will steer you to the geographical outlet nearest you. Here is what you get from Beckley-Cardy:

1. Just about any kind of teaching material or office supplies a church could ever need.

2. Prices lower than you will pay anywhere else for the same thing, because of the thousands of schools they supply, making possible for them to produce in such vast quantities that prices are kept lower.

Broadman Press. Some of their products have been described elsewhere in this book. Strong in audio-visuals.

Concordia Publishing House. This publishing voice of the Lutheran Church, Missouri Synod, includes in its pages the best products of other publishers, as well as their own. In addition, they publish separate small catalogs in specialized areas, such as films and filmstrips, which may be requested along with the large catalog.

David C. Cook Publishing Company features some unusual teaching aids of their own, besides listing some outstanding aids from school suppliers. Their catalog, however, will not take the place of Beckley-Cardy, since Cook's is 72 pages and Beckley-Cardy's about 800.

Gospel Publishing House has some interesting and innovative methods featured in their resource materials.

Moody Press has in their reliable books and superior filmstrips some of the most helpful material available. Their motto "A Name You Can Trust" justifiably inspires confidence in what you order.

Nazarene Publishing House has a big catalog which lists materials from many publishing houses, including school supply places. Instead of "pushing" only their own materials, they make available the best from a number of reputable houses. You will find that their music arm, Lillenas Publishing, provides high quality resources.

Regal Books is the book publishing arm of Gospel Light Press, a pioneer Sunday School curriculum publisher. Their materials are from the pens of age group specialists. They are also contemporary.

Scripture Press is another pioneer of Sunday School curriculum publishing. Their materials are not a duplication of others, but are fresh from the pens of experts in their fields. Victor Books is their books division.

Zondervan Publishing House is another old and trusted

name in Christian publishing. Besides good books with Bible background and Bibles with usable maps, Zondervan has some pictorial works in the area of Bible Geography, which will be listed in another part of this chapter.

Library Resources

Subject Guide to Books in Print, annually brought up to date, will list available books in any specific area of interest.

Reader's Guide to Periodical Literature likewise indexes articles in magazines. Any librarian is happy to explain the use of reference books which cannot be removed from the library.

Books—Archaeology and Bible Background

An Archaeologist Looks at the Gospels, by James L. Kelso (Word Books) is a 1975 paperback. Kelso's book *An Archaeologist Follows the Apostle Paul* is also a 1975 paperback from Word. Both these volumes are written for the layman. That means the text is written concisely and with interest. There are dozens of pictures throughout. Kelso's explorations have given him a firsthand acquaintance with the excitement and thrill of piecing together the culture of long ago people through finding the outlines of buildings and the everyday implements and adornment of the people.

Archaeology in Bible Lands, by Howard F. Vos (Moody Press), 1977, is a technical book in layman's language. The science of archaeology is explained, together with its importance to the Bible student. One section is devoted to description of the archaeology of ten different Bible lands, with reference to contemporary digging as well as past accomplishments. The volume is well illustrated by photos as well as reconstruction drawings in art.

Archaeology of the New Testament, by E. M. Blaiklok (Zondervan), 1970, has six chapters concerning the Life of Christ and five pertaining to the balance of the New Testament. One discusses the Dead Sea Scrolls. Profusely illustrated, the book is written so a layman can understand and enjoy it. Some obscure Scriptures are explained in the light of recent findings.

Baker's Pictorial Introduction to the Bible, by William Deal (Baker Book House), is an inexpensive source of pictures of Bible places and customs.

Bible History Visualized, by Ray Baughman (Moody Press), is an amazingly simple but graphic inexpensive paperback that is a nutshell wrap-up of Bible History, from Genesis to Revelation. Using an outline of titles beginning with the letter *C*, the author provides a framework for good visual presentation and retention. Sixteen chapter titles (as Creation, Confusion, Captivity, Consummation) hinge the essential facts around the key word. Charts are given throughout the text, to make facts seen at a glance. There are line drawings which can be used as ideas for overhead transparency projection. This is a handy book for every teacher.

Cities in New Testament Times, by Charles Ludwig (Accent Books), is an illustrated paperback which makes twelve first-century cities vibrate anew with life. Its companion, *Rulers of New Testament Times*, presents colorful stories about the lives and reigns of the Herods and the Caesars to help your understanding of the times in which Christ lived.

Wycliffe Historical Geography of Bible Lands, by Pfeiffer and Vos (Moody Press), considers the lands of the Bible, one by one, and discusses their history, customs, significance and archaeological discoveries about them. Clear pictures accompany every section. If a student of Bible Geography could own but one larger, more expensive book, this is a likely candidate.

Zondervan Pictorial Bible Atlas, by E. M. Blaiklok (Zondervan), is another fine volume of the more expensive variety but worthy of a place in every teacher's library.

Books—Life in Bible Times

Daily Life in Bible Times, by William Sanford LaSor (Standard Publishing), paperback, is still in print. It is described on the title page as "Study Course for Youth and Adults." It would be a great text for an elective course in Sunday School on Bible backgrounds, but it is also good reference for the Sunday School teacher who wants to understand some of the many phases of Bible Geography and life it covers.

Everyday Life In Bible Times is *National Geographic's* beautiful compilation of some of their great articles on the

Holy Lands. The book includes such chapters as "The World of Abraham," "The World of Moses," "The World of Jesus," and "The World of Paul." Illustrated by full-color (and sometimes doublespread) pictures, the book provides a clear view of the land and its people. Archaeological discoveries are cited, showing their clues to the lives of the kings and people who lived there long ago. This is a real armchair trip.

Good News, The Story of Jesus, by Jim Comstock (EPM Publications) is a real novelty book. Using the newspaper tabloid size and format, Comstock presents facts played up in news style. The articles are illustrated by pictures of people dressed authentically like the Bible characters they depict. Even the "ads" are of products that would have been necessary and desirable in those days. Write to the publisher for special rates for quantities of five or more to one church. Well worth each teacher owning.

Life and Times of Jesus the Messiah, by Alfred Edersheim (Wm. B. Eerdmans), is a "golden oldie." Its author has long been recognized as one of the foremost scholars of Palestinian lore. It is, however, more pedantic than the more recent books listed, in the author's evident desire to explain everything fully. The author also wrote *Sketches of Jewish Social Life in the Days of Christ,* reprinted also by Eerdmans, but no longer listed in *Books in Print.* It may be obtainable from a library.

Manners and Customs of Bible Lands, by Fred Wight (Moody Press), is outstanding in its clear presentation of facts about Bible people and their manner of life in the various lands. Obscure references become clear as background is here given. Drawings also add to the value of this work.

Handbook of Bible Lands, by Guy P. Duffield (Regal Books), is arranged in alphabetic order by place names. The author gives information about the place as given in both the Old and New Testaments. Considered a good handbook for travelers, it is also valuable reference for a teacher.

Halley's Bible Handbook (Zondervan) is a compact source of many facts about the people and places in every book of the Bible. The author also gives information about archaeological discoveries.

The New Testament in Living Pictures, The Old Testament in Living Pictures, both by David Alexander (Regal), provide outstanding photographs of Bible places. Some are panoramic views and others are close-ups. Maps are included to give perspective.

Strange Scriptures That Perplex the Western Mind, by Barbara M. Bowen (Eerdmans), is still in print. The author clarifies customs and words that are often obscure to the average layman.

Books—Fiction

Just a note here for the more prolific readers among us. Some of the most realistic and accurate Bible background information may be found in the books of such authors as Frank Slaughter, who is careful and accurate in his research. His *God's Warrior* (about Paul) and *Road to Bithynia* (about Luke) attest to this fact. He cites his sources, which are among the best. If fiction cites real places, it must provide real facts. For some, those facts will be more readily assimilated in a story form.

Books—Teaching Methods

While most of these books have been included in the chapter where they are especially pertinent, we will list here some which are most useful to teachers of Bible Geography.

Bible Things to Make and Do with Boxes, by David W. Thompson (Standard), presents instructions for making chariots, a sheepfold, an altar, Palestinian house interior—and many more—all out of boxes.

Equipment Encyclopedia, Handcraft Encyclopedia, and *Visual Aids Encyclopedia,* all by Eleanor Doan (Regal Books), contain patterns and instructions for making objects to depict Bible places, people and customs. They should be in every library.

How to Make and Use Overhead Transparencies, by Anna Sue Darkes (Moody Press). The title is self-explanatory, and details are given in the chapter about the Overhead.

Projectable Bible Atlas, by Anna Sue Darkes, is a new product produced by the author's company, Faith Venture Visuals. It contains five base transparencies, 19 overlays and 48 paper masters, and costs $49.95.

Teaching Tools You Can Make, by Lee Green (Victor Books), is a gold mine of ways to use everyday objects to make teaching aids: mailing tubes, plastic bags, 35mm film cans, old shoestrings and milk cartons are among the dozens of "raw materials" listed.

What's in the Bag, by Marie Chapman (self-published; may be ordered from author for $1.50 postpaid). This looseleaf book has eight chapters of ways to use a lowly brown bag in Christian education. Among other useful Bible models are instructions for Palestinian houses and the tabernacle.

Magazines

Aramco World Magazine (Arabian American Oil Company), is a beautiful full-color magazine, printed on the finest stock of slick paper. It is full of articles and pictures that are rich in Bible background. It is the house organ of this vast oil corporation, whose headquarters are in Saudi Arabia, right by the Persian Gulf. Even the news about the oil company itself will have pictures typical of the land. You may receive the magazine by writing Public Relations Director, and request it, explaining your interest in the study of those lands. They state that the magazine is "distributed without charge to a limited number of readers with an interest in . . . the history, culture, geography and economy of the Middle East." It is bimonthly.

Evangelizing Today's Child (Child Evangelism Fellowship, Inc.), often has pictures and stories with Bible background.

National Geographic (previously identified and described).

Sunday School Action and *Sunday School Counselor* are both publications of the Gospel Publishing House in Springfield, Missouri, whose catalog was listed.

Sunday School Lesson Illustrator (Baptist Sunday School Board). This quarterly magazine has biblical background articles to go with the current Sunday School lessons. Write for ordering information.

Sunday School Times and Gospel Herald prints fictionized stories of Holy Land visitors, with true facts and color illustrations. A nice way to take an armchair tour.

Success (Accent B/P Publications) is a Christian education magazine that prints suggestions for making classes interesting, including the study of Bible backgrounds.

Teacher's Swap Shop is a monthly paper for teachers, obtainable for the asking. They will tell you how to stay on the list. Each issue has ideas for making review and drill actual fun. They also publish a half dozen different compilations of valuable ideas which they have printed over the years, with 101 ideas in each book.

LIST OF SOURCES

Abingdon Press, 201 Eighth Avenue, S., Nashville, TN 37203

Accent Books, 12100 W. Sixth Avenue, P.O. Box 15337, Denver, CO 80215

American Bible Society, 1865 Broadway, New York, NY 10023

American Mission to the Jews, Angel Memorial House, 149 Avenue B, New York, NY 10009

Arabian American Oil Company, 1345 Avenue of the Americas, New York, NY 10019

Baker Book House, 1019 Wealthy Street, Grand Rapids, MI 49506

Baker's Plays, 100 Chauncy Street, Boston, MA 02111

Balda Art Service, 710 West Fifth Avenue, Oshkosh, WI 54901

Baptist Book Store, 110 Broadway, Nashville, TN 37234

Baptist Sunday School Board, 127 Ninth Avenue, North, Nashville, TN 37234

Beckley-Cardy, 1900 N. Narragansett, Chicago, IL 60639

Bible Land Slides, P.O. Box 434, Stayton, OR 97383

Broadman Press, 127 Ninth Avenue, North, Nashville, TN 37234

Carpenter's Workshop, Tel Aviv, P.O.B. 3321, Israel

Connie Champlin, 2051 N. 54th Street, Omaha, NE 68104

Marie M. Chapman, Route 5, Box 170, Amherst, VA 24521

Child Evangelism Fellowship, Inc., P.O. Box 348, Warrenton, MO 63383

Concordia Publishing House, 3558 S. Jefferson Street, St. Louis, MO 63118

David C. Cook Publishing Company, 850 North Grove, Elgin, IL 60120

Eerdmans Publishing Company, 255 Jefferson Ave., S.E., Grand Rapids, MI 49502

EPM Publications, 1003 Turkey Run Road, McLean, VA 22101

Faith Venture Visuals, Lititz, PA 17601

Friendship Press, 475 Riverside Drive, New York, NY 10027

GAF Corporation, P.O. Box 444, Portland, OR 92707

Giant Photos, Box 406, Rockford, IL 61105

Gospel Light Publications, Box 1591, Glendale, CA 91209

Gospel Publishing House, 1445 Boonville Avenue, Springfield, MO 65802

Gospel Services, Inc., P.O. Box 12302, Houston, TX 77017

Hammond, Inc., Maplewood, NJ 07040

Japheth Press, Ltd., 6 Harkevet Street, Tel Aviv, Israel

Milliken Publishing Company, 1100 Research Blvd., St. Louis, MO 63132

Moody Press, 2101 W. Howard Street, Chicago, IL 60645

National Geographic Society, P.O. Box 1806, Washington, DC 20013

Nazarene Publishing House, P.O. Box 527, Kansas City, MO 64141

Prima, Hudson Photographic Industries, Inc., Irvington-on-Hudson, NY 10533

Regal Books, Box 1591, Glendale, CA 91209

Scripture Press, 1825 College Avenue, Wheaton, IL 60187

Standard Publishing Co., 8121 Hamilton Avenue, Cincinnati, OH 45231

Success Magazine, 12100 W. Sixth Ave., P.O. Box 15337, Denver, CO 80215

Sunday School Times and Gospel Herald, P.O. Box 6059, Cleveland, OH 44101

Teacher's Swap Shop, P.O. Box 777, Taylors, SC 29678

Through the Bible Publishers, 6441 Gaston Avenue, Dallas, TX 75214

Union Gospel Press, P.O. Box 6059, Cleveland, OH 44101

Victor Books, 1825 College Avenue, Wheaton, IL 60187

Visuals, 440 N.W. 130th Street, Miami, FL 33168

Warner Books, 75 Rockefeller Plaza, New York, NY 10019

Wolfe Worldwide Films, P.O. Box 25900, Los Angeles, CA 90025

Word of Truth A-V Ministry, 2977 Hillcrest Road, Schenectady, NY 12309

Word of Truth Productions, Box 288, Ballston Spa, NY 12020

World Prophetic Ministry, Dr. Howard C. Estep, P.O.
  Drawer 907, Colton, CA 92324
Wright Studio, P.O. Box 19201, Indianapolis, IN 46219
Zondervan Publishing House, 1415 Lake Drive, Grand
  Rapids, MI 49506